BOATS, SMOKE, STEAM AND FOLK

EXPLORING THE CANALS OF THE WEST MIDLANDS

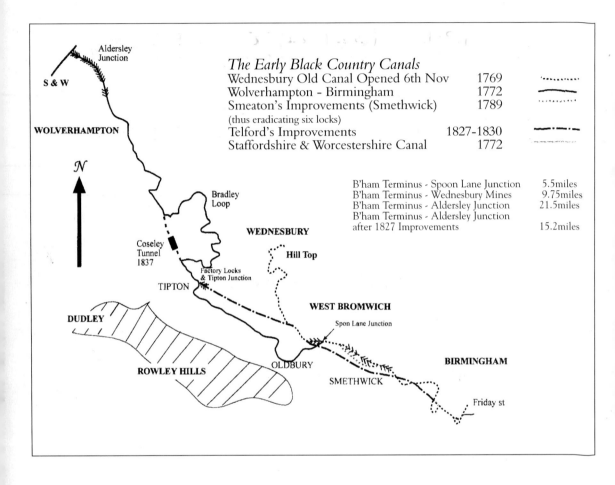

The Early Black Country Canals

Wednesbury Old Canal Opened 6th Nov	1769	·············
Wolverhampton - Birmingham	1772	──────
Smeaton's Improvements (Smethwick)	1789	··········
(thus eradicating six locks)		
Telford's Improvements	1827-1830	─·─·─·─
Staffordshire & Worcestershire Canal	1772	

B'ham Terminus - Spoon Lane Junction	5.5miles
B'ham Terminus - Wednesbury Mines	9.75miles
B'ham Terminus - Aldersley Junction	21.5miles
B'ham Terminus - Aldersley Junction after 1827 Improvements	15.2miles

Aldersley Junction

S & W

WOLVERHAMPTON

N

Bradley Loop

Coseley Tunnel 1837

WEDNESBURY

Hill Top

Factory Locks & Tipton Junction

TIPTON

DUDLEY

WEST BROMWICH

Spon Lane Junction

ROWLEY HILLS

OLDBURY

SMETHWICK

BIRMINGHAM

Friday st

BOATS, SMOKE, STEAM AND FOLK

EXPLORING THE CANALS OF THE WEST MIDLANDS

ROBERT DAVIES

TEMPUS

First published 2001

PUBLISHED IN THE UNITED KINGDOM BY

Tempus Publishing Ltd
The Mill, Brimscombe Port
Stroud, Gloucestershire GL5 2QG
www.tempus-publishing.com

PUBLISHED IN THE UNITED STATES OF AMERICA BY:

Arcadia Publishing Inc.
A division of Tempus Publishing Inc.
2 Cumberland Street
Charleston, SC 29401
(Tel: 1-888-313-2665)
www.arcadiapublishing.com

Tempus books are available in France, Germany and Belgium
from the following addresses:

Tempus Publishing Group   Tempus Publishing Group
21 Avenue de la République   Gustav-Adolf-Straße 3
37300 Joué-lès-Tours   99084 Erfurt
FRANCE   GERMANY

British Library Cataloguing in Publication Data.
A catalogue record for this book is available from the British Library.

ISBN 0 7524 1765 7

Typesetting and origination by Tempus Publishing.
PRINTED AND BOUND IN GREAT BRITAIN.

Contents

Acknowledgements

This publication could have not been possible without the help of many people, and I would like to thank: Phil Clayton of the B.C.N.S. for reading my manuscript and giving much advice. John Brimble and The Tipton Civic Society for information on the Tipton Town trail. All those who were good enough to sit for interviews including Dennis Fellows, Phil Garrett, Jack Garrat (no relation) Margaret Wood and the tapes of her late husband. The three Bumble Hole chaps, Jack Edgington, Joe Chilton and William Jones. Fred Heritage. Colin Williams for sitting for hours, pouring over maps and photos. Keith Hodgkins for photos. Ruth Collins for photographs from her father's collection (William King). John Allen, for giving me his work on the Horseley Iron Works. Len Crane for the information on the pumping station at Bratch – and photos. George Price, for his help with Cobb's Engine house. Brian Thompson, for taking me on a tour of the Bradley workshops, and for supplying the photos at Ocker Hill, and Jack Jenkins for his memories of that depot. And finally, my wife Jane, for help with the wild flowers, and doing the excellent pencil drawings.

Sources of Photographs other than those already mentioned.
The Black Country Living Museum. pages 23, 38, 51, 73
Smethwick Library pages 20, 34, 70

A New Form of Transport

Narrow boats, coal, steam engines, tunnels, locks, bridges, horses, aqueducts and the lives of thousands of men women and children, came to be wrapped up with what was for Britain, a whole new transport system. Certainly, canals had been used before, but never had a complete inland waterway *system* been developed on such a grand scale, one that would empower the industrial revolution.

In the grand scheme of things, 200 years is a relatively short piece of time. Yet within this time frame, an amazing form of transport was developed, grew to a prosperous zenith, went into decline, and virtually disappeared.

When I started to explore this strange watery world, I wanted to understand the motivation behind this amazing network and to know the answers to questions like – When was it built? Who did all the work? Who made those lovely cast iron bridges? Why are there two tunnels under Dudley? How were they excavated, and what tragedies occurred in that dirty, dark and back-breaking experience? How did those huge, powerful steam engines work? Who designed them? What was their connection with the canals? What was it like to work on the canal itself, doing repairs, or moving stuff about?

These are some of the questions that I have attempted to answer in this book, aided by the experiences of the men and women who actually worked them (though in the twilight years of the system it must be said). I hope therefore that this account will not be lifeless history, with a collection of interesting facts and unusable data, but rather that the information and walks featured within these pages, encourage you, the reader, to get out there, and perhaps boat, walk or cycle this 200-year old transport system. To actually go through the tunnels, run your hands across those gracefully designed iron bridges, and to imagine the sights and sounds of a bygone age, with blast furnaces roaring, and mighty steam engines thumping away.

Maps, like windows into the past, are extremely valuable for getting the historical feel of an area, and when several maps of the same place, but from different years, are placed next to each other, the fascinating development of the landscape can be perceived. Some of those maps have been reprinted, others redrawn, so that the development of a specific area can be seen. Photographs also play a major part in telling the story, but note that most of the old black and white photographs in this book were not taken by professionals, but by amateurs with inexpensive cameras. Some are small, others a little cracked because of being carried around in a pocket for thirty years. Nevertheless, as instants in historical time they are priceless.

Our first consideration is that of speed. When we consider the speed of modern transportation, it seems amazing that such a slow form of transport as the canal could ever have been envisaged, let alone developed. In fact it is impossible to understand why the canal was ever born as a mode of transport, until you have a picture of the condition of the roads in Britain during the seventeenth and eighteenth centuries. In retrospect it could be said that had someone come along and invented the pneumatic tyre and tarmac, the canals would never have been. So the question is, were the roads really that bad?

Road Transport

During the middle ages, the manor was responsible for the maintenance of the roads in its area, though the word road is a little misleading, those highways were very often simply dirt trails, closer to what today we would refer to as a bridleway. As time went by and manorial influence waned, the parishes took over the role of road 'maintenance', which in simple terms, meant raking over the surface and then tipping on top, a layer of stones and grit. After a few days of British weather and only light use, these 'roads' were soon reduced to ruts and potholes, making the use of heavy wheeled vehicles almost impossible.

In Britain during the 1750s, a steady stream of the general population moved away from the countryside to the rapidly expanding towns and cities, where there appeared to be better opportunities for employment. London, Manchester, Leeds and Liverpool were all growing in size and population. Birmingham and its satellite towns at the heart of the country, was becoming a manufacturing centre thanks to the natural resources of coal, iron ore, limestone and clay. Bulky and heavy raw materials and finished goods were being transported on the backs of horses and mules, large carts were out of the question. So every day there was a steady flow of these beasts of burden in and out of the city, and it was this traffic that added to the poor state of the roads.

The Duke of Bridgewater was trying to solve the problem of getting coal from his mines in Worsley, to Manchester, less than twentymiles away. He was impressed with the canals he saw on his tour of the continent, and was set to have his own built. Plans were made and James Brindley was drawn into the scheme because of his practical ability. Brindley had much experience with water mills and had recently designed and built a water channel on the river Irwell. As well as building a canal, they planned to connect the underground coal workings, by water, with the canal. The workings were to be served by small boats, 47ft long by 4ft wide, the forerunners of the ubiquitous narrow boat.

Leading industrialists in the Midlands, like Josiah Wedgewood, and James Watt and Matthew Boulton in Birmingham, noted the success of the Manchester scheme. They realised that a canal was the solution to their transport problems, and quickly set to the task of raising support, financial backing, and the necessary government approval for such a huge undertaking.

Thus Britain entered into a period of widespread and intense digging activity that historians call 'Canal Mania', a time when the government granted acts for numerous canal enterprises. Brindley's initial plan was extremely far sighted. He wanted to create a network of waterways that would link the four major rivers of England, the Mersey, Severn, Trent and Thames, thus serving the inner landlocked areas of the Midlands. He soon came to be employed by several canal companies, acting as surveyor and general engineer. It was impossible, however, for him to be in a dozen places at once, and other men came to be in charge of specific sections after the initial line had been agreed.

By 1769 the Bridgewater canal had been operating for four years, and hundreds of miles of canal throughout the country were either being planned or dug. The tough excavation work was all undertaken by primitive means – picks, shovels, and wheelbarrows, along with the construction of bridges, wharves, aqueducts, locks and tunnels. Large gangs of men were gathered to do this back-breaking toil, many of them coming across from Ireland due to the dire economic conditions in that land. These rough gangs of hard working men came to be known as Navvies (after navigators) and the canals were referred to as the navigation's. In this same year, the first canal in the Midlands was opened. It was the section between Wednesbury, with its rich coal seams, and Birmingham. Instantly the price of coal halved from around fourteen shillings a ton to about seven. The first boats into the city were greeted by grand celebrations, bell ringing and brass bands, the long trains of coal-bearing mules were soon to be a thing of the past.

In 1772 the stretch between Wolverhampton and its junction with the Wednesbury canal opened, making a route between Wolverhampton and Birmingham. Even though the canal at this point terminated in Birmingham, the city was destined to become the hub of the inland waterway system.

Below is the advertisement in *Aris's Gazette* – The Birmingham newspaper of the time – announcing the original scheme.

BIRMINGHAM, Jan. 24 1767
The Utility of a Navigable Cut from the Wolverhampton Canal, through the Coal Works, to this Town, having been pointed out in a proceeding paper, by which (exclusive of the other Emoluments) it appears that the Town will reap a considerable Advantage in the Maintenance of its Poor, a meeting, for the further Consideration of this scheme is thought essentially necessary; therefore the Constables, Churchwardens, and Overseers, do hereby give public Notice, That a Meeting will be held on Wednesday next, at Six o' Clock in the Afternoon, at the Swan Inn in this Town, at which the Gentlemen and Inhabitants are solicited to attend, in order (if the Scheme shall be approved) that a proper Person be appointed to Survey and give an Estimate of the Canal in Question, and that such other proposals may be offered as may seem most likely to answer the intended Purpose.

The Earliest Midland Canals

These two early canals formed the start of what eventually became the B.C.N. or Birmingham Canal Navigation's, though the Wednesbury Old Canal, never actually reached Wednesbury town, it terminated in the higher ground around Hill Top, eventually being known as the Balls Hill Branch.

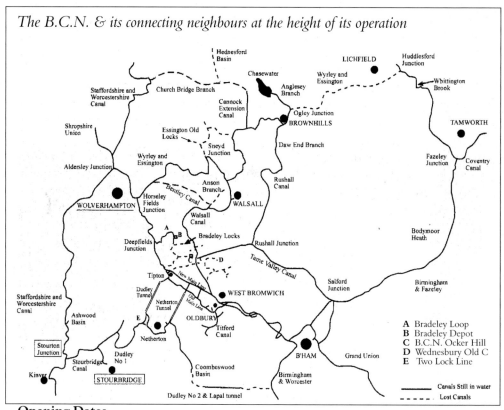

The B.C.N. & its connecting neighbours at the height of its operation

A Bradeley Loop
B Bradeley Depot
C B.C.N. Ocker Hill
D Wednesbury Old C
E Two Lock Line

——— Canals Still in water
- - - - - Lost Canals

Opening Dates

Wednesbury Canal	1769	Digbeth Branch	1799
Birm - Wolv	1772	Chasewater Res	1800
Staffs & Worcs	1772	Smethwick Cutting	1829
Trent & Mersey	1777	Birm & Worcs	1815
Dudley No.1	1779	Coseley Tunnel	1837
Ryders Green Locks	1786	Island Line	1838
Dudley Tunnel	1792	Tame Valley	1844
B'ham Fazeley	1794	Netherton Tunnel	1858
Wyrley & Ess'ton	1797	Cannock, Ext	1863

Early maps, such as that appearing in The Gentlemen's Magazine of 1771, show a representation of the original route. Our drawing however is taken from a later one-inch-to-the-mile map of the system as it was actually built, and used right up to the Second World War. After that, many miles of the B.C.N. were lost due to lack of use and land redevelopment. Most of the Wednesbury Old Canal and the loop around Coseley have since disappeared, but small sections of the original routes, are still to be found and enjoyed as they were. Another early survey map of 1767, broadly similar to the one that appeared in the Gentlemen, showed that Brindley originally envisioned a tunnel under the high ground at Smethwick. But after boring several test pits, they discovered sandy soils and other obstacles, making a tunnel out of the question. The canal was therefore taken over the summit by means of the twelve locks shown. Six of them are still extant, and are among the oldest locks in the Midlands. Some of the heavy oak required for the lock gates, came from local trees, near the Oak House in West Bromwich.

The meandering course of the James Brindley route is plain to see. As the crow flies from Wolverhampton to Birmingham it is exactly eleven miles, by canal it was over twenty. This route was chosen to keep it close to

Aldersley Junction – the gateway from the B.C.N. to the Staffordshire and Worcestershire canal, and then on to the busy waters of the river Severn at Stourport. Now a secluded leafy scene, Aldersley's character is far different from the junction it was a hundred years ago. Then it was thick with traffic, going in and out of the Black Country. A time when both canal companies had their toll houses here. But this splendid red brick bridge is still the entrance to the twenty-one locks that make their steady march up to the Midlands plateau, a rise of 132ft. In 1998 Dennis Fellow's boat had suffered from engine troubles, and I gave him a hand to bow-haul (hand haul) it through these locks. It was hard work and I gained an insight into the graft of previous generations.

The Staffs & Staffordshire & Worcestershire canal is forty-six miles long and runs from Great Haywood – near Stafford, where it connects with the Trent and Mersey canal. It flows in a roughly North-South route to Stourport, on the river Severn, passing the busy town of Wolverhampton.

Above is a view of the two Wolverhampton – Birmingham lines, near Smethwick High Street, separated by only a few yards and 20ft in differing levels. The top level is part of the short addition that Smeaton made in the late 1700s. The restored pumping station that topped up the higher canal stands between the two lines.

the contours, though there were objections to its construction from some landowners. Early canal design favoured the contour method, because it saved the heavy and costly work of deep cuttings and lengthy embankments (a later development). There was another advantage to a wandering canal though. It meant that many more of the Black Country mines, iron works and factories could be accessed. The section from the Wednesbury coal fields into Birmingham was the first to open, and the boats with their precious cargoes of coal, from the Spon Lane area, were unloaded at Friday street amidst great celebrations.

There were problems at the Smethwick summit from the start, due to water shortage and congestion at the locks. James Smeaton was called in at the end of the eighteenth century, to see what could be done, and he made a lower line at 473ft, so that six of the highest locks could be completely done away with.

Note that in these early years, Birmingham was a terminus. It was not until later that it become a through route for the Fazeley, Warwick, Grand Junction and Birmingham – Worcester canals. It took four and a half years to complete the two canals opposite. On 27 September 1772, just as a general assembly was sorting out Brindley's payments, he became ill and died. Some say he was totally overworked by the enormity of the canal projects that he was in charge of.

Exploring The Old and New Main Lines

This walk, looking not only at the rich historical legacy, but also at the diversity of the natural world to be found, includes its wild flowers, birds and insects.

As they weave their silent and often unnoticed course through towns and cities, canals often provide a green corridor where a wide variety of wild flowers, insects, birds, shrubs, trees and small mammals can be found. Deep cuttings like the Galton Valley, which is truly man made, can boast a greater number of species than their rural rivals, and are worth investigating, savouring and simply enjoying. So this pleasant little trail, set deep in the heart of the old Black Country provides historical contemplation, and nature's little gems.

Our route starts just outside West Bromwich, a few yards from Sandwell's rail station in Bromford Lane. Bromford Iron Works, on the canal side, is one of the few remaining iron works left from the heavy industrial days of the nineteenth century. The Birmingham-Wolverhampton Main Line is easily accessed from Bromford Bridge, a recent concrete structure. Technically, we are now on a piece of the Old Wednesbury Canal of 1769, before it was incorporated into Telford's improvements of the 1830s. On the towpath we were greeted by one of many buddleia bushes, but on this particular day there were no butterflies, though there were Tortoiseshell and Peacocks in the area.

I was on this occasion, accompanied by my wonderful wife Jane, who doubles as my personal wild flower and bird expert (this saves me the trouble of carrying at least two books). We had chosen an excellent piece of weather in July, and had decided to spend most of the day on this walk, taking sandwiches, and ready to check out every nook and cranny. July is a pretty good month for wild flowers, which have been displaying since late May.

Myriads of sticklebacks caught my eye first, they seemed to be skitting just under the surface. Sticklebacks, I concluded must be hardy little creatures as they cope with water that could hardly be termed fresh. In springtime, the male takes on a shiny green hue with a red chest, and sets about building the nest, using water weeds and a mucus that he manufactures inside his diminutive body. Fortunately (for other aquatic life) the stickleback is small, if he were any larger he would be the terror of the deep. Did you know that these strange little fish like to be tickled along their backs? Go on give it a try (Just don't let anyone see you, especially if you talk to them at the same time).

How clean this water is I cannot say, but I did see here a few weeks previous, a whole school of enormous carp, making their slow course toward Tipton.

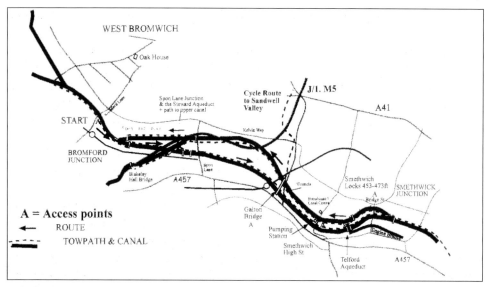

Starting from Bromford lane, this circular walk to Smethwick Junction is four and a half miles, though it can be shortened at several intersecting points. The map at 30mm to the mile, shows the two parallel canals some distance apart. This has been drawn so to aid clarity, in fact the canals are never farther apart than a few hundred yards.

Between the pumping station and Telford Aqueduct they are only 10-20yards apart, separated of course by the 20ft embankment.

And when this section of the canal was drained for maintenance during the later summer months, there were thousands of large black mussels on the canal bed, a positive sign surely. We made our way around the first bend toward Bromford stop – the island in the middle of the canal just prior to the junction. The original octagonal toll house which graced this island has long gone, its position now occupied by a thriving colony of Red and White Clover, while Yellow Ragwort and Hedge Mustard grew to the right of the towpath. Broad-leafed Willowherb meanwhile clung tenaciously between the gaps of the engineering blues at the water's edge, and close by there was Scented Mayweed with poppies adding a dash of red to the border.

Teasels were coming close to maturity at the edge of the towpath, with their ridge of spines following the centre of each leaf (underneath) And all this before the first bridge! On the opposite bank, for many yards was a stand of silver birch, and the large white trumpets of bindweed waved gently in the breeze, mixed as they were with the ever-present pink of Rosebay Willowherb and bramble.

Around the first bend, comes Bromford Junction, with the canal forking left up the Spon Lane locks to the 473ft level, while Telford's canal carries straight on. The junction is of course greatly enhanced by two bridges from the Horseley works. The one on the right was cast in 1848, the left one in 1828, and if you look at the side castings you will see samples of a two section, and three section bridge. While I savoured the use of the bridges, running my hands along the smooth guard rail, Jane was busy adding to the wild flower list, and she showed me the spiked yellow-green flowers of the Wild Mignonette. There was only one sighting of this lonely species, its roots firmly wedged between the canal's coping stones, though there were several examples of Great Burnet Saxifrage. The umbellifer just mentioned, resembles many of its family members, and at times identification can take some effort, the difficulty being added to by the fact that sometimes you come across local variations on a theme (all very confusing and time consuming as you wade through your guidebook).

At this point we swapped towpaths to continue along to the Steward aqueduct, a heavy, blue brick, two-arch structure, built to carry the old Brindley line across to its junction with the original Old Wednesbury canal. The Steward aqueduct, as an engineering piece, is greatly dwarfed by the M5, which opened to traffic in 1970, and five huge supports go straight down into the centre of the canal to carry this colossal motorway. However it is difficult not to marvel at both of these two very different buildings. The contrast between them is obvious, the dark, gently dripping melancholia of the 1829 structure emanates from a totally different architectural stable to its overhead concrete companion. During 1999 the Steward aqueduct required some remedial work, and Morrisons were called in by British Waterways as contractors to put things right. At least two cracks in the structure were causing leaks, and much of the facing brickwork needed re-pointing.

If you look carefully at the aqueduct, you will notice that like many canal bridges, it is built on a skew, and not at 90 degrees to the canal underneath. This makes for a much more complex structure, as bricks cannot be laid to a level. Looking at the courses of brickwork in the arch, they can be seen heading away from the limestone blocks at a considerable angle. Skilled bricklayers are therefore necessary to do this kind of work, as they often have to rely on their eye, and not a set line. And if you examine the aqueduct, there isn't a straight line to be seen anywhere. Also notice the slightly longer blue bricks, and the comparatively tight joints (three eighths of an inch) compared to modern gauging. The bond is generally English, where a stretcher course is followed by a course of headers.

To hold the aqueduct together for another two hundred years, the men were drilling horizontal holes, three metres into the structure, to put in steel rods. Around the rods is a kind of sock, and when this was in place, a grout was pumped at pressure around the rods to bind everything in place. There are nine rods for each arch. The grout had a secondary purpose, it would be forced into all the internal cracks and crevices, and thus seal any leaks. The bricklayers in charge of the pointing up (replacing lost mortar from between the bricks) had been instructed to point up with the same mortar that had been originally used on the structure in the late 1820s, a lime mortar. During the last fifty years or so, all building has taken place with cement, making a very hard bond. English Heritage have requested in recent years that a mortar that builders have used for centuries, relying on the binding power of lime, alone should be used. Leaving the M5 and the Steward aqueduct behind, we discovered Bittersweet and Tufted Vetch growing at the base of the tall retaining walls at the left of the towpath. I particularly like the bittersweet flowers with their purple petals and bright yellow thrusting centres.

The next two bridges originally provided access for the firm of Chance Brothers. This once-large site was world famous for its glass, and supplied the complete glazing for the Crystal Palace in London. A few yards further on, as we gradually went deeper into the grand cutting, we came across the sunny lemon and orange flowers of the Common Toadflax. Like many other plants it had taken root right at the water's edge, and it amazes me how plants develop and thrive amidst the narrowest of cracks. Along the left wall, the dull purplish heads of Hemp Agrimony were well established. This colony continued several hundred yards to the deepest part of the cutting, showing how plants move along the canal corridors by the differing means at their disposal. Some simply have their seeds blown along the towpath, others drop into the canal and drift with the gentle current until they find suitable lodgings, while many grow new plants from their extended root system.

We then entered the deepest part of the valley and stopped for a bite to eat, sitting on the grassy banks at the edge of the towpath. We tried to imagine what it was like when this amazing place was dug in the 1820s, when the valley would be full of pick-swinging navvies. I looked at my hands to conjure up images of the worker's calloused and bleeding palms, as they slaved for their coppers. The view then would have been dirt, barrow runs, and more dirt. But now, 150 years later, those same banks have been taken over by nature and abound with colour and greenery. When in season, the gorse and broom provide a wonderful yellow glow to these precipitous banks, but this month our eyes were caught by the pretty

Bromford Junction - Horseley Bridges - Spon Lane Bottom Lock.

grasses, from where a hundred grass hoppers chirped soothingly to each other. One variety of grass was truly difficult to describe, its thin waving stems were pink, but the seed heads that topped each stalk were a creamy straw colour, so that as you gazed at a whole patch of the stuff from a distance, there was an indescribable blending of the two hues.

Mixed in with the bushes and grasses we found Yarrow and Black Medick, which is a strange name for a plant with yellow clustering flowers. As Jane was finishing her final sandwich, she drew my attention to the tiniest blue flower I have ever seen. There was only one of its type, and it was hiding amongst other plants right by her feet. With a flower head about 3mm across, it sported the most delicate blue petals, with pointed green sepals between. Our book identified it as Wall Speedwell. Not more than a few inches away, was the tiny white flower of the Field Mouse Ear, and when you get the chance to feel its basal leaves, you will see why it has this unusual title.

Where are all the Insects?

Buddleia bushes were again in evidence, but still no butterflies. An orange skipper settled next to some large thistles, and it was then that we spotted the Burnet Moth, or should I say Burnet Moths, for there were several.

Hovering a few millimetres above the head of the thistles, they make a striking sight with their black wings and bright red spots. Just around the corner came the ponderous blue brick bridge that carries Roebuck lane over the canal, and Smethwick's rail station is on the right bank. I suppose that this bridge has merit in its own right, but it does obscure somewhat the most famous bridge of all. Suddenly there it was in front of us, the Galton Bridge, in all its glory, like some graceful metallic rainbow, with its well proportioned diagonal bracing and slender hand rail.

The cycling organisation Sustrans (sustainable transport) have taken a cycle route from this point, and a well designed pathway leads up and away from the bridge. This route (No.5) goes through Sandwell Valley and then, after passing under the Newton road, joins the Tame Valley canal, close to the junction with the Rushall canal. So get yourself a bike and have a go, its a pleasant way of connecting the two canals, and exploring Sandwell Valley at the same time.

After passing through the Galton Tunnel (lower) we arrived at Brasshouse bridge, though the large industrial brass-making premises that gave this road its name have recently been razed and levelled. The late nineteenth century pumping station sits next to it, and has been well restored by volunteer canal societies and the council. The station pumped water from the lower to the upper level via two Tangye pumps (a local firm). Proceeding along the towpath, in the direction of Birmingham, we next encountered the Gothic grandeur of the Engine Arm Aqueduct, sometimes called the Telford Aqueduct. This unique and attractive aqueduct, with its pointed arch shapes certainly wouldn't look out of place in a church, and I think it's rather wonderful. At this point you can walk up the slope to the upper canal, though if you're feeling fit you can continue to Smethwick Junction and come back via the three Smethwick locks.

If you take a look at the Top lock you can just discern where the remains of a second flight of locks started. These were part of John Smeatons improvements of the late 1700s, when an attempt was made to improve the flow of the very busy boating traffic at this time.

On the higher 473ft level we are essentially heading back, parallel with the lower New line, toward our starting point. After Brasshouse bridge is passed again, the old canal, for a few hundred yards at least, takes on an almost rural scene, with coots attempting canal-side nests, as it winds around the wooded mount. Here we found Hedge Woundwort and Ribbed Melilot. I like the extremely rough old limestone wall that borders this pleasantly wooded section.

Only a few boats lock up into this ancient bit of canal, but thankfully you come across the odd one or two intrepid types who can't resist the challenge, and help to keep it open and in use. After the Summit copse, a second concrete tube, twin to the one below, is encountered. Both were placed there to provide foundations for the new road above.

After emerging from the tunnel, on the right, are the remains of the coal loading chutes of the Jubilee Colliery, while at the left of the towpath are the ruins of a little hut that the boatmen used to use as a shelter. After that there is a final bit of rurality, before we are brought crashing back to modernity by the ominous presence of the M5. The motorway straddles the canal along this section, directly over the Spon Lane Junction, supported by a veritable forest of substantial concrete legs. The motorway is only thirty years old, but is already in need of serious maintenance, and this section is being tackled in the millennium.

To the right of the junction can be seen the striking red brick exterior that used to be the thriving concern of Kenricks. Looking more like an old boys grammar school, this once tasteful piece of Victorian architecture seems rather sad sitting under the gaze of the M5.

Swap towpaths at Spon Lane Bridge.

Down Spon Lane locks we go, noticing the unique split bridge at the head of the top lock. The scrapyard to the left is a bit of an eyesore, certainly no fitting tribute to what is probably the oldest set of working locks in the country. My copy of West Bromwich history, reminds me that the oak timbers for the original gates, were cut from the vicinity of the Oak House less than a mile away. The Oak House, owned and run by Sandwell Council not far away, is a rare example of a half timbered-building with its lantern tower still extant. The Oak House can be easily accessed

The Telford / Engine Arm Aqueduct (Horseley).

(admission free) from Bromford bridge, continuing left along Kelvin Way, then turning right up Albion Road / Oak Lane.

Our little trip is now almost over, and we find ourselves back at Bromford Junction. Jane and I finished off with a couple of photographs, and marvelled at the swallows and swifts as they wheeled low across the water, like a bird's version of the Battle of Britain.

Below is a listing of the wild flowers we found on that day alone. How many can you find?

Ragwort

Broad Leafed Willowherb

Hedge Mustard

Tall Rocket

Poppies

Scented Mayweed

Teasels

Red/ White clover

Bindweed

Wild Mignonette

Great Burnet Saxifrage

Bittersweet

Hemp Agrimony

Tufted Vetch

Common Toad flax

Yarrow

Black Medick

Field Mousear

Wall Speedwell

Ribwort Plantain

White Foxglove

Hedge Woundwort

Ribbed Melilot

Meadow Vetchling

Rosebay Willowherb

Creeping Thistle

Sandwell Park Colliery Loading Station, West Bromwich. Notice the inclined plane, bringing the coal tubs down to the canal side. They have now gone, but remains of the concrete coal chutes are still to be seen, as can the remains of the hut just off the nearside towpath (see Galton Valley Walk for location, off Brindley's Old Line).

Old King Coal

When the Wednesbury Old Canal opened to traffic in 1769, the carriage of coal was its first and main concern. Even though the canals came to carry all manner of other goods like iron, building materials and foodstuffs, coal always reigned supreme. While these materials were carried in their tens of thousands of tons, coal eventually – during the Victorian period, went into the millions of tons. The stories of the canals and of coal are very much bound up with each other, though the story of coal began millions of years before, with the death of the primeval forests. In recent times, as one industry flourished so did the other, as one died so followed its mate. Therefore the majority of people interviewed in this book were connected with the coal trade.

When the Romans came to Britain they had to contend with a Midlands covered by the last in a very long line of dense natural forests. They penetrated this often boggy and wild treescape with a track that became Ryknield or Icknield street, some parts of which can still be traced in the south of Birmingham and Sutton park. However, long before the legions made inroads into wild and wet Britain, a variety of coal seams had been laid deep down underground, by those much earlier forests, awaiting the attention of future generations. Generations who would find a ready use for this hard black rock.

By Tudor times, much of this forest had been cleared, and coal started to be used in small quantities, for mainly domestic purposes. Much of the coal was to be found near the surface, requiring only picking, but shallow bell pits were sometimes used. The people living in places like Wednesbury, Tipton and West Bromwich had stumbled on to the tip of an industrial iceberg – vast hidden quantities of fuel. The removal of this shiny carboniferous material was to dominate the lives (and deaths) of thousands of British folk for over 200 years.

In places the seam was thirty foot thick and was known locally as the 'thirty foot seam'. On maps it delineates what came to be 'The Black Country'. It almost seems that this untapped resource was waiting for the industrial revolution – and the canals and boats to carry it to its varied destinations.

By the late 1600s, Birmingham was growing as a manufacturing centre for metal goods. A hundred years later, after the American war of independence, a Frenchman called Faujas de Saint-Foud visited the town, and was greatly impressed by the 'Ironmongery' there. He said 'It was made in greater perfection, with more economy, and in greater abundance than anywhere else' and attributed this ' modern miracle of manufacture, to the abundance of coal, which had created in the midst of a barren desert, a town with 40,000 inhabitants, who live in comfort, and enjoy all the conveniences of life'

Perhaps his comments are a little over the top, but he was echoed in 1791, by Arthur Young who wrote, 'All the activity and industry of this kingdom is fast concentrating where there are coal pits; the rest of it has but one object, which is the cultivation of the soil, and to open as immediate a market, with coal and manufacture, by means of inland navigation as possible' The industrial race was well begun.

Whereas the majority of folk only managed to scrape a meagre living out of coal, leading industrialists, and a handful of landowners, especially those who owned property and thus the mineral rights where coal and other raw materials could be found, made a fortune. One of such families were the Dudley's who resided at Himley Hall, and their coal and iron mines, lying in the Swinford and Pensnett Chase estates, were mentioned in records as early as 1639. Those same mines were still producing well, sixty years later, in 1701. During this year, we can have a glimpse at the accounts for just three of the collieries owned and run by this wealthy family. They are the Knowle Hill (Netherton), Paddock, and New Park pits. Receipts for coal for that twelve month period were £857 11s 9d, £447 0s 3d and £540 5s 11d respectively. There is no doubt that these three pits were extremely valuable to his lordship, who incidentally earned an approximately equal amount from the agricultural side of the business. With the coming of the canals (and Lord Dudley was a prime supporter) these pits increased their value. Lord Dudley owned twenty pits within a three mile radius of Stourbridge alone.

As mentioned earlier, before the 1600s, coal was easily taken from outcrops near to the surface, and then from shallow pits. But the eighteenthth century saw a steady increase in the use of deep workings. Coal at the surface was often of inferior quality, and deeper and deeper pits were required to get at the higher grades, and quantities of coal. These included the Bloomfield (Tipton), Horseley, Wednesbury and Bagnalls collieries. Now the pits were going down beyond 200ft, and a new problem arose, that of underground water.

A patent for a Savery engine was taken out in 1698, and the first factory for the manufacture of large steam engines was set up in London in 1702. Wednesbury was one of the first towns to receive one and put it to use. It was placed to drain a low-lying piece of ground called the Broad Waters, and the adjacent mine. This early engine proved almost useless, not so much a problem of design, but more of poor manufacture. It was Newcomen who really designed and built an effective steam engine, one that would prove useful to the miners, and pump all of the water out of their mines. One of the first of his engines was set up in 1712 somewhere near the present day Black Country Living Museum.

By 1800, canals, steam engines and collieries, were all working in concert. In 1791, when Arthur Young visited Birmingham, he estimated the town's annual consumption of coal to be 200,000 tons. In time the iron industry alone was to consume an amazing 1,750,000 tons per year, mostly transported by canal.

The Canal Carriers

Several decades after the emergence of the inland waterway system, cargo carrying companies started to make their presence felt. Fellows Morton & Clayton started in the Black Country and were one of the big players.

James Fellows of West Bromwich got the company moving in 1837, and in those early days he tended to concentrate on the long distance trade. Many of those journeys were to and from Brentford, utilising the Grand Junction canal (now the Grand Union). By 1855 his boats alone were transporting over 13,000 tons of iron each year between Birmingham and London.

One of his early bases was at Toll End, Tipton. In 1860 James' son Joshua took control of the family business. After trading as Fellows Morton & Co. for some years, in 1889 it finally became Fellows Morton & Clayton. The boats used at this time tended to work in pairs and were horse drawn. Their boats when loaded, showed little freeboard and were easily identified by the simple black and white colour scheme, but later in the 1920s they had a complete makeover and bright colours were introduced. The background colour was red, with yellow and green bands with white lettering. The painting was generally done with finely ground matt paints with a high gloss varnish on top.

A busy scene at F.M.C.'s Birmingham Depot, early twentieth century.

The lavish sign writing gave the company name, boat name and fleet number. F.M.C was definitely one of *the* great canal carrying companies, but even they could not compete with the railways, and the burgeoning road transport industry. of the early 1900s. They went into voluntary liquidation just after the Second World War in 1948, after trading for just over 100 years.

As an addition to being a carrying firm, F.M.C built their own boats to their own specifications, and tried various means of boat propulsion, including steam. Several steam-powered boats were added to the fleet, but the disadvantage of this form of power was the weight of the steam engine and its fuel, thus resulting in freight reduction, and there was no mass conversion.

The Fly Service

High value goods, especially those of a perishable nature, needed to be moved as quickly as possible, and the fly boats concentrated on this facet of the trade. The fly boats were a faster, non-stop craft that continued travelling right through the night, the horses being changed at regular stages along the way. The boats themselves had a different hull design, built for speed, having a rounded section rather than a flat bottom, and the prows and stern tended to have a greater rake, enabling them to improve their cut through the water.

Cargoes were normally well under the usual tonnage (less than twenty tons), and they enjoyed certain privileges over other boats. They had priority in entering locks, and slower craft were to drop their towropes when they saw the fly boat approach. Also as a means of identification they sported a black roundel on a white background at the front of the boat.

A typical B.C.N. Toll house.

F.M.C. operated a steam powered fly service between Braunston and Birmingham, Leicester and Nottingham. On other runs the boats were horse powered, but by the 1930s, all boats on the Grand Union (formerly Grand Junction) were powered. The company's main horse depot was at the hub of the canal system at Birmingham's Liverpool Street, not far from the Fazeley Street wharf. At this depot there was continual employment for the local saddlers and smiths, and interestingly they had their own individual horse feed that included in each ton. 8.5cwt of hay, 2cwt of straw, 1.5cwt of bran, 1.5cwt of peas, 2.5cwt oats, and coloured confetti, which was added to discourage theft.
(cwt = a hundred weight)

Born on the Canal. Fred Heritage

Fred Heritage was born in 1936, on a narrow boat in the Wolverhampton area, and like thousands of children born on the move, this is as specific as it gets. That year however was destined to be one of the last peaceful years that Britain and Europe were to enjoy before the outbreak of the Second World War. Fred's Parents both worked and lived on the narrow boat *Carp* and they were employed by a firm of carriers that has now become synonymous with the inland waterway system, that of Fellows, Morton & Clayton. (F.M.C.) They were to continue working for this firm throughout the war years.

The *Carp* however was under-powered, and Fred's father decided to swap it for the narrow boat *Adder* which had a 15hp Bolinder engine. This step-up in power enabled the family to tow an extra boat (a butty) that no doubt Mrs Heritage would steer. The *Adder* in its turn, was exchanged for the n.b. *Peacock*, still extant and to found sometimes in the Black Country Museum near Dudley. Narrow boat cabins had changed little over the years and a ten foot by seven foot cabin, at the rear of the boat served as a complete home for Fred, his mum and dad, and his older brother. Between those small walls was a fold down table, a cupboard and some shelves. There was a small black cooking range which was coal-fired. It comprised an oven, with room on top for a few saucepans. A few feet away was the family bed, classed then as a double but, by today's standards, it was probably only slightly wider than a modern single.

When most people think of the canal carrying trade in the Midlands they tend to jump to the conclusion that it was all coal and bricks, but in the late 1930s and early 1940s F.M.C. were hauling the sort of goods that we now get in our local Tesco trucks. This included canned and bottled food and drinks, cheese, and tea and coffee, usually packed in wooden cases, though grain was in sacks.

F.M.C. by this time were well organised and had depots all over the country, especially in large towns like Nottingham and Liverpool, and Fred remembers calling in at the local ones at Wolverhampton and Birmingham, as well as those in Manchester and Ellesmere Port.

The Birmingham depot was situated on Cambrian wharf, a short arm that led off from the Farmers Bridge flight of locks in the town centre. Now the wharf is only twenty yards or so in length, but during the war it continued for several hundred yards to a terminus at Baskerville House. A few pages on is the fully developed canal system in the centre of Birmingham. One interesting account of the development of this area, concerns the celebrated Mr Baskerville, who had made his money in the printing trade. He was an eccentric by nature, in life and in death. In his will he requested that he be buried at the bottom of his garden, upside down and under the windmill.

Not long after his burial, the ground needed to be dug up to make way for the canal and wharf. Mr. Baskerville's body was so well preserved after exhumation, that a local put it on display in a shop window – until it was removed as being inappropriate.

Present-day Baskerville House commemorates this eccentric Birmingham character, and a font named after him is represented at the front of this grand building with enormous concrete and metal stamps.

Returning back through time to the 1940s and Cambrian wharf, we envisage a busy scene with narrowboats being loaded with a great variety of goods. Most of this loading and unloading was done by hand, but there were a few small petrol and hand driven cranes to assist, and a restored one can be viewed today, on the towpath outside the Flapper and Firkin pub. As soon as the Heritage's boat was loaded, off they set along the new main line for Wolverhampton, the Shropshire Union canal, and their final destination Ellesmere Port. A typical working day started at around six. The family would wash, using water from a water can filled from either a water point or spring en route, have a cup of tea, a bite to eat (small children had ostermilk) and off they would go. Mr Heritage was paid for a complete journey, therefore it was in his interests to work long hours and make as many miles a day as possible.

On the return trip, they would bring back copper or spelter into Birmingham, making a two way trip of five to six days, payment for which was around five pounds. In 1949 Fred's mum and dad went to live in one of the houses owned by the new British Waterways, a few yards from the Tividale aqueduct.

When Fred was fifteen he started working for B.W. on general maintenance duties, including towpath work and lock stoppages, but he spent a total of thirty-two years on the dredger, working with a group of men on that very necessary but unglamorous job of clearing muck and rubbish from the murky waters of the local canals. Now, at the start of the Millennium, Fred is in retirement, but he busies himself doing volunteer work for British Waterways and is often seen with the restored boat *Atlas* at waterway events around the country.

Broad St Tunnel in the 1970s before, redevelopment.

Passengers & Parcels

Generally speaking, we tend to associate the activity of narrow boats – especially in the Black Country – with the business of cargo carrying, usually of coal, iron and other bulk materials. So it is surprising to learn that there were in places regular passenger (plus parcels) carrying craft, known as packets. C.S. Forester, in one of his novels about the fictitious seafaring character of Horatio Hornblower, sets at least one chapter to such a journey during the year of Nelson's death (1805)

In the Midlands though we had a larger than life character, by the name of Thomas Monk, who ran among other ventures, a regular packet service on the Birmingham Canal Navigation's. Thomas Monk, born in 1765, was only a teenager when the canal age was in full swing, but he was quick to grasp the potential of this new technology. His predecessors had been barge builders, in the rapidly expanding town on the Severn at Stourport. Thomas however became much more interested in the narrow boats that were coming down into Stourport along the Staffs & Worcestershire canal. This interest was to take him into the boat building and carrying businesses, and Thomas is credited with the development of cabins at the rear of the narrow boat. These cabins were, over time, to evolve from a crude shelter and storage area for animal feed, into living quarters (albeit tiny) for a man and his wife, and in many cases, several children.

T Monk Advert

Thomas had eight sons (only one daughter) who he trained in the boat building trade, and this enterprising man ultimately became responsible for running a fleet of 130 boats. His great-grandson, a Mr John Mills, gives us some interesting insights into his great-grandfather's character, relating an event when some of his boats were detained in London due to a labour dispute. Without waiting for any more details, Thomas – a man of action – was off along the towpath (a distance of around 140 miles) to sort things out. Thomas was a doer, not just a talker. A hard worker himself, he expected his men to also work hard, but equally, when work was short, he wouldn't see any of his employees go without, he would assist them financially and even feed them. The business grew, and his boats were so identifiable that they came to be called 'Monkey boats', a term that stuck with the canal people for many years.

But, returning to our theme of passenger transport boats, we read in an advertisement from a Midlands newspaper, of Thomas Monk's boat 'The Euphrates Packet' and its three day a week run, from Tipton to Birmingham. This service, starting in the early 1820s was to run for the next twenty five years. When it started, the short-cut of Thomas Telford's Island line, from Tipton to West Bromwich, hadn't been built, and the route was therefore along the old main line, with stops at Tipton Green, Dudley Port (Dudley Port has of recent years moved from its original location, to where the rail station now stands), Tividale, Oldbury, Spon Lane, Smethwick and Winson Green, with its terminus at the Waggon & Horses – Friday Bridge, Birmingham. A ticket was one shilling and sixpence (first class).

This journey, of nine and a half miles, was scheduled to take two hours, which by all accounts was pretty quick. There were three locks encountered on the way, and if you allow ten minutes per lock, which is itself fast, then this alone consumes half an hour. And even though the *Euphrates* had a sleek hull, and was pulled by a team of horses, they must have been travelling at six miles an hour at least. I have no doubt that it was quite an exciting journey into work and back. Nevertheless, with four hours of travel in one day, it does seem to point a finger at the poor state of road transport at that time, even between these two well-developed towns in the mid 1800s.

The *Euphrates* extended its journey twice, first as far as Coseley, when the start point was Wallbrook, and a newly established inn was named 'The Packet Inn'. Perhaps that is where the Black Country phrase 'I wish yode packet in ' comes from'. Ten years later the complete route went all the way from Wolverhampton and on into Birmingham.

Thomas died at the age of seventy-nine, in 1843, and was suitably buried in 'St Thomas's churchyard, Dudley. The Black Country lost a notable character, and only a few years later, the work of the packet boats came to an end with the opening of the Stour Valley rail link in 1852.

Birmingham – Branches and Wharves

The accompanying map helps us to see how the canal system was established in central Birmingham, along with its wharves, basins depots and warehouses. The time shown is the early twentieth century, a time when the canal-carrying era had passed its peak but was still complete, and very much alive.

The Birmingham Canal Navigation's Company Offices at the turn of the century. They were situated on Suffolk Street, opposite Paradise Street. The two archways shown, saw much activity, with a continual stream of horse drawn carts that went to and from the two parallel basins behind. (see map on following page) The B.C.N. at its height had a trade of some 8.5 million tons per year, much of that in coal to the brickyards, foundries, furnaces and other industries that filled the Black Country.

Notice the octagonal centre building that set the style for the much smaller toll offices throughout the B.C.N. Also the curved outer wing walls and beautiful glass balls for the gas lamps. These buildings had been demolished by 1930, and the Central TV studios now stand in their place.

The very first termini are shown on our earlier map, and were at Friday Street, on the Newhall Branch, and Brick Kiln Piece (which roughly corresponds with what is now Gas Street Basin. That was the situation during the latter half of the eighteenth century, when Birmingham was the end of the line. However developments such as the Birmingham / Worcester, Fazeley and Birmingham & Warwick canals over the next fifty years would transform Birmingham from a navigational cul-de-sac, into the hub of waterway operations, controlled from the main offices of the B.C.N.

At the left of the map we see the old Brindley line of 1772 coming in from Wolverhampton, past the New Union Flour Mill and then veering around to the Junction by Kingston Wharf. From this junction it went south east to Gas Street Basin, made a turn and terminated in two long basins at the B.C.N. Offices, opposite Paradise Street.

The first junction is noted in some books as Farmers Bridge. The B.C.N. Society have a finger post calling it Old Turn Junction, another source has it as Deep Cutting Junction, I'll stick with the B.C.N.S's version. The horse shoe stables, an interesting piece of circular brickwork, owned by the railway company are still extant, and now next to a popular pub in the heart of Brum.

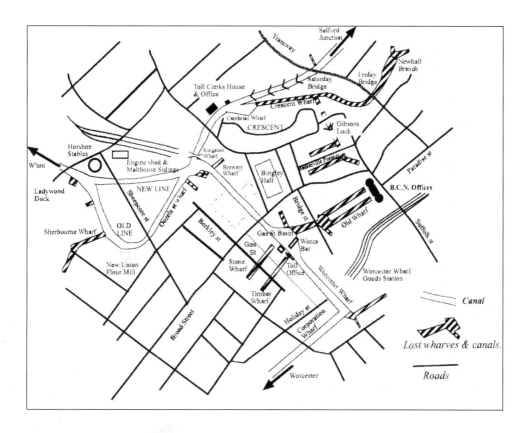

Coal being unloaded into the heart of Birmingham. Looking up the Oozels Loop (by Sea life Centre).

Gas Street basin during the war years. Notice the church that was built over Broad Street tunnel.

From early days wharfage was always a problem for two main reasons, one was the length of the boats themselves (70ft was taken up every time a boat moored), the other was due to the slow and primitive means of loading and unloading. In 1812, the construction of new wharves helped to ease the problem for a while. The tunnel from Crescent Wharf led to Gibsons Arm, and Baskerville Basin. These wharves were slightly higher than the 1772 level of 453ft, and Gibsons Lock was built to raise and lower the boats. A steam pump was employed to maintain the upper level.

As late as the 1700s, Birmingham was still very rural in appearance. From this time onward, as Birmingham grew, and the canal became connected to more towns and cities, the land became extremely valuable, and was quickly sold and developed. By the 1880s the whole area was filled with industrial buildings or warehouses, its rurality lost forever. Farmers Bridge, the bridge near to the top lock at Cambrian Wharf, was named after a local land owner, James Farmer.

From the 1920s onward, there was a steady decline in the use of narrow boat transport. The canal was losing trade to the railway and the improving road network. Wharves and arms that previously bustled with activity, now saw fewer and fewer boats, until they eventually closed. The Newhall branch and Crescent wharf closed in 1926, the arms leading up to the B.C.N. offices two years later.

The B.C.N. Committee at Halesowen. Jack Jenkins is almost certain that this boat was the Selene, *and kept for the special use of the bosses at Ocker Hill.*

The Gas Boats

The photograph below shows Thomas Clayton's boat yard at Oldbury, located on the Old Main Line, close to the junction of the Titford branch canal. Note the flush decks of the boats, with Stour nearest. At this busy depot there were areas for stabling, feeding and watering the horses, fodder stores and a manure heap (great for the garden). At least one full time blacksmith was employed, not only shoeing the horses but also making repairs to the boats.

To assist in unloading the boats, a wooden barrel, filled with concrete was lowered onto the gunwales to give it a list. The fluid cargo could then be completely pumped out, as it flowed to one side. William Clayton started out in the canal-carrying business in a modest way in 1842. From an early base at Salford Bridge (Birmingham) around 1856, Clayton operated mainly long-haul transport of such items as timber, paving stones and clay drainage pipes. After an initial expansion to a boatyard at Saltley on the Birmingham Warwick Grand Junction canal their main cargo was still timber, but a start was made in transporting tar. Later, a trade was developed with the local gas works of removing the liquid waste mentioned earlier, and the 'Gas Boats' were born. To this was added the transport of crude tar. In 1889 Clayton's merged with Fellows Morton & Co. However, the heavy liquid trade was kept as a separate concern, and it continued to be run by William's grandson, Thomas. At this time, Thomas moved the centre of the carrying trade to the base below.

Clayton's Boat Yard – Oldbury

By 1935 the addition of a boat repair yard was made in order to carry out the ongoing maintenance of a fleet of narrow boats that was now eighty strong. Clayton's used mainly horse-drawn craft right up to 1937, when in May of that year they purchased their first motor boat *Soar*.

While much of Clayton's trade was Midlands-based, to and from the local gas works, they did start a regular run to Shell's refinery on the Manchester Ship Canal, via the Shropshire Union canal. Petroleum products were brought all the way to Shell's depot at Langley Green (near Oldbury) and the 160 mile return journey took a week. The gas trade has of course completely gone, as has Clayton's boat fleet, but at least one boat, the *Giffard* has been restored in memory of this company, and is owned and run by Edward Paget Tomlinson who often supplies artwork for the canal press. Phil Clayton reminds me that the Stour can also still be seen in a much altered form.

One of the last Gas Boats. This time a charming young lady is at the helm of Giffard *as it heads for Oldbury. Notice the dog and kennel on the deck.*

One of Clayton's boats, Spey, *struggling through the iced waters of the Old Main line to get back to base.*

Stewponey and its Toll Office

Margaret Wood, now in her seventies and living in Kingswinford, worked for the Staffordshire & Worcestershire Canal Company at Stewponey Wharf during the Second World War. Stewponey Lock is only a short distance from Stourton Junction, a mile or so west of Stourbridge. The busy A449 runs past one side of the lock, while on the other the Stour Brook flows, all three taking a generally parallel route north-south from Wolverhampton to Kidderminster.

Margaret has memories of a busy time during the last war, with a constant flow of narrowboats through this particular lock. After working for a while in service at Stourton Castle (just up the lane) Margaret moved employment to this brisk little post on the S&W. She also met her future husband George, who also worked on the S&W doing a variety of jobs.

After getting married she started in the toll office, where a daily record was kept of every narrow boat that passed through the lock. The office itself is now converted into a house which is still extant. The small octagonal building which could easily be mistaken for the toll office was in fact used by the boatmen during the war years as a small canteen, where cups of tea and sandwiches were served (spam and cheese were popular).

Other buildings close to the toll office included a warehouse, carpenters shop and stables for twenty horses, and it was George who worked in these stables during weekends, with the unenviable task of mucking out, feeding and watering the animals. During the week his employment included piling, lock repairs, dredging and hedge cutting.

The toll office was by today's standards extremely bare, supplied only with a plain wooden desk and chair, and a ledger for the day's entries. At the close of the day's proceedings, the completed sheets would be placed in an envelope and posted off to the S&W offices in Wolverhampton. Information on these sheets related to the type of goods carried (e.g. coal), time, tonnage, name of boat and steerer. As soon as a boat came into the lock Margaret would be there, as the men were loath to hang around. They would quickly take their ticket from Margaret's hand and be off.

Much of the canal trade flowing through Stourton in the war was coal, heading for the Stourport power station. As a youngster in the 1960s I recall seeing the station, its chimneys still covered in wartime camouflage to protect it from German bombers. Cargoes entering the lock may have come from Ashwood Basin or Littleton Collieries and T.S. Element's boats were frequent callers. Other goods on the S&W included vinegar from Stourport and carpets from 'Kiddy'. The occasional horse-drawn 'Fly' boat made its appearance.

When boats were closely following each other, or going in opposite directions, and happened to come to the lock at the same time, this was often a recipe for squabbles and disputes, especially if one man decided to try and jump the queue. During the early war years, traffic on the Staffordshire & Worcester canal was pretty constant throughout the week. Boat numbers coming into Stewponey lock was between twenty and thirty per day, and Margaret worked from 6.00 a.m. to 6.00 p.m.

Quite often the flow of boats was in one direction, and then later on the same day, boats would come back empty on the return trip from Stourport. It was only in later years that motor boats towing butties made their appearance. Gauging did not actually take place at Stourton, but Margaret, after a little experience, could tell at a glance how much weight was on the boat. Later, small red and white metal plates were fixed by the company to the side of the boats as a loading indicator. The company started this practice because some boatmen in their desire to get a little more speed out of their craft, would shovel quantities of coal into the canal, and then make up the weight with water as they got close to Stourport. If they were caught doing this – and some were – it was instant dismissal.

A fine example of a boatman and his working horse, equipped with the necessary tackle for boat hauling. Hector Daniel Duffield, after being made redundant from Beans Foundries in Tipton, decided to go into coal carrying, and set himself up with the horse 'Sandy'. The gentleman on Hector's right is Clarence Brown who worked for the family firm of Elwell & Brown, also based in Tipton.

The Kinver Light Railway was a busy transport link before and after the Second World War, bringing workers out from the Black Country and Stourbridge to work on the canal, and there was a regular service from Stourbridge, passing Stourton, crossing the canal, and on into Kinver, its final destination. The village of Kinver, from way back in Victorian times, was still proving to be a popular day out for folk from the Midlands conurbation, and thousands were using the KLR for their picnicking days out.

Once a year during the summer months, the committee boat *The Lady Hatherton* (like the *Seline*, which was used by the B.C.N. committee at an earlier time) would make her slow course along the Staffordshire & Worcestershire canal, carrying the company directors and major shareholders. This leisurely boat ride, taken over several days, enabled them to cast a keen eye over the company's assets, and have a fine old time in the process. Each morning a convoy of chauffeur-driven cars would deposit their charges at the moorings of the *Lady Hatherton* and off they would go, checking out the towpaths, buildings, locks and employees.

George Wood, Margaret's husband, born in 1928, started working on the Staffordshire & Worcestershire canal with his father, prior to the last war. His father's job was mainly with the spoon dredger, and they could be found anywhere along the forty-six mile stretch of the canal. Weekly pay around this time amounted to about £2 5s, with 7s 6d going in rent. George recalls both mules and donkeys being used for boat haulage, but horses were much preferred.

George's grandfather also worked on the S&W, but as a bricklayer, being concerned with lock wall rebuilds and bridge construction. One tale that George related, was when his grandfather was rebuilding bridge no.55 near Castle Croft farm. The foundations from the earlier bridge had been left as a base, so new brickwork was laid on top, and then the old bridge was knocked away. Essentially this technique differed little from building a bridge from scratch, but in the original circumstances, a timber centre would have been used to support the brickwork until set. On this particular day, to get to bridge 55, George's grandfather had to walk nearly ten miles from Stourton, carrying his bag of tools, before even starting work. He happened to be thirty minutes late, and the company suspended him for three days.

Lock repairs, where brickwork had become so bad it needed replacing, usually took place at the weekend, when traffic was minimal. The men would start as soon as possible on the Saturday, and have it all knocked out, rebuilt and pointed up ready for reopening on the Monday morning. Ice breaking went on here as it did throughout the waterway system. On the S&W the men started work at a very cold five o'clock. One boat would work on the section from Gailey to Stourport, while the Northern ice boat worked from Great Haywood down. If the weather demanded it, a boat ran throughout the night, making an already dangerous job even more uncomfortable.

Birds, Beasts and Iron Works

A short walk along the Staffordshire & Worcestershire canal from Kinver to Stourton, and back, taking in the resident wildlife, and a brief look at its history. Total distance – just under four miles.

Some walks can be savoured over again, and in any season, this is one of them. A little observation applied along the way, can prove fruitful and rewarding. At the height of summer, this very pretty meandering stretch of the Staffordshire & Worcestershire canal, is rich with greenery, wild flowers, and the gentle hum of busy insects. In autumn, the gold and red hues of the transforming leaves, contribute to a different flavour, while a crisp but bright wintry day, with a smattering of ice and frost, brings forth a completely new dimension.

Kinver is a good starting point, next to the Vine pub. The weather on my last visit was glorious, with deep blue skies, a huge bonus if you're bent on taking a few photographs, or simply enjoying the delicate colour of the flowers and insects. A long line of colourful narrowboats thronged the section of canal leading up to the first bend, and the sun glinted from a glossy surface that was littered with a million fairies (dandelion seeds). Overhead a buzzard with its mewing cries, made full use of the thermals to gain height – our first bird. The sweet scent of blossom came softly on the breeze, while from the trees came the see-sawing notes of the chaffinches.

Prior to the coming of the canals, Britain's rivers and streams were the focus of industrial activity, when the mills and forges made the most of the ready water supply to provide power. Only later when steam power came along was there a shift toward places like Birmingham. But here at Hyde lock on the Staffs & Worcestershire canal, only a few miles from Kinver, a substantial iron trade had already established itself on the banks of the Stour Brook.

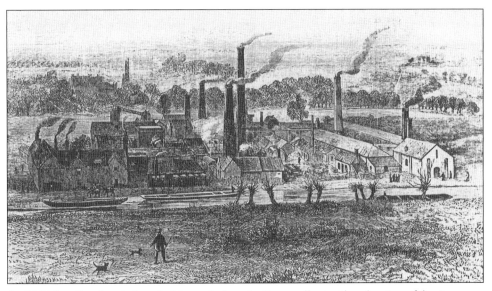

In 1772 Brindley cleverly brought his canal along the Stour valley to take advantage of the rivers contours. Lee and Bolton's Hyde Iron Works (above) quickly developed a canal frontage, with a short arm into the works.

Today the buildings have gone, nature has taken over, with woods and tangled undergrowth. Pleasure craft now passing this pretty lock, would find it hard to imagine that a huge industrial base had ever existed.

Jane and I walked away from Kinver lock, leaving it and the waterworks buildings behind, with their boreholes going down some 750ft. We were quickly immersed in a narrow verdant corridor, with dappled light, filtering down through a canopy of leaves onto the surface of the dark green water. The soft 'putt-putt' of an approaching boat at the first bend mingled pleasantly with the peaceful buzz of busy insects. On the left the enormous leaves of the Gunnera grew low, punctuated with Red Campion, while on the steep right bank Foxgloves emerged proudly from the twisted and tangled roots of trees. A wren flitted through the mixed woodland of oak, beech and ash, which were thirstily drawing up water from the natural edge of the canal, their emerald boughs cascading down from on high to the water below. Along the hedgerow we discovered Comfrey, sporting both purple and white flowers. Close by were Common Figwort and Hedge Woundwort with their lovely purple /pink lipped flowers, and Yellow Flag Irises, with their feet firmly in the water. At Hyde lock Jane found a small clump of Monkshood with its beautiful blue hooded flowers, but be very careful with this plant, every bit of it is poisonous.

At Stewponey lock we rested a while and sat on the balance beam, while my daughter Lauren became fascinated with the water rushing down the circular weir that is a unique feature of the Staffordshire & Worcestershire.

I tried to imagine what it may have been like during the Second World War when Margaret Wood worked here as Toll Clerk. No pleasure boats in those days – except the *Lady Hatherton*. Just a steady flow of working boats with mainly coal to Stourport Power Station, though there were also cargoes of carpets from Kidderminster, and vinegar out of Stourport.

Margaret met George, just before the Second World War, when she was a house maid, up at the castle. Every sunday, she passed the Stewponey wharf on the way to church, and George noticed the regularity of this pretty girl in blue. So on sunday he timed his work schedule at the stables so that he could simply say 'Hello' as she passed. The 'hello' grew into chats and conversations, and at length they got married. After living at the house at Stewponey for a while, they moved to the house at Rocky Lock.

From Stewponey lock we walked the short distance to the secluded Stourton junction, where four lock chambers take boats steadily up toward Brierley Hill and the Black Country. An extremely tall Perennial Sowthistle stood in the hedgerow with the delicate yellow flowers of Herb Bennet lurking below. The beetroot red of Hedge Woundwort was also close at hand, while Blue and Great tits could be heard in the adjacent woodland that surrounds the junction. Our eyes were caught however by the sudden glint from the wings of a Banded Demoiselle that flitted overhead, and then landed delicately on the lush green vegetation by the water's edge.

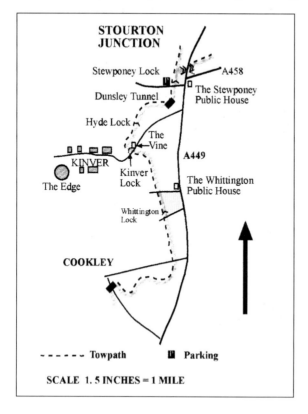

A map from the 1940s – which even today would represent Stourton as a very small rural community.

We then turned and retraced our steps, passing the steady gaze of the huge Stewponey pub that sits on the road junction, and then through one of only two short tunnels on the Staffs & Worcs, at Dunsley (the other is at Cookley). Dunsley tunnel cuts through one of the many sandstone outcrops along this stretch of canal, and even though most of the interior of the short tunnel displays the original workings, some brickwork has been added to provide strength. Near Dunsley Hall in 1805 the Squire of Dunsley Hall was waylaid and robbed by a highway man who left him for dead. The squire was definitely not dead however, and managed to crawl back to the hall. The highwayman was caught at Whittington Inn (on A449) not far away, publicly hanged and gibbeted at Gibbet Wood. He was the last man in England to suffer this penalty.

We stopped again at Hyde Lock for photographs, where a Damselfly made a fleeting appearance. A hundred years ago, Hyde Iron Works, where all manner of iron goods were made,was next to this lock. The works was here well before Brindley brought the Staffs & Worcs this way, and like its neighbours it utilised the waters of the River Stour, that traces a parallel course, only yards away. Nevertheless nature has almost eradicated this piece of intensive industrial activity, and all that remains is a house near the towpath. From Hyde lock our nature walk was made complete, with a quick blue flash from the resident Kingfisher, though it must be said that these birds are extremely shy and the best time to catch them is early in the morning, when few people are about. From here, it was back to the welcoming arms of the Vine and Kinver.

BIRDS and INSECTS

Robin
Blackbird
Wren
Buzzard
Blue and Great Tits
Kingfisher
Song thrush

Chaffinch Banded Demoiselle Damselfly
Common Blue damselfly
Butterflies were absent on this day

FLOWERS

Foxgloves
Common Figwort
Perennial Sowthistle
Red Campion

Monkshood
Flag Iris
Herb Bennet
Hedge Woundwort

Birmingham Canal Navigation Depot
Ocker Hill

Just after the Second World War, prior to nationalisation, the Black Country canals were run by the B.C.N. At this time a young Colin Williams went to work for the company at its Ocker Hill depot as an apprentice carpenter. The depot, just off present day Ocker Hill island, almost opposite St Marks church was an important pumping station on the B.C.N. It was situated on a piece of high ground, at the termination of a branch that connected with the old Bradley loop. Even at this late stage of canal usage, there were still in water, dozens of arms that had served the mines, factories and foundries for a hundred years. Water for this particular arm, was pumped up from the much lower Walsall canal, a few hundred yards away, via an underground culvert (see diagram p46).

Besides being a very important pumping station, the depot's function was to produce most, if not all of the timber products that the company required, from windows and doors to lock gates. The B.C.N. employed about twenty men at Ocker Hill at this time, and there were areas and buildings set aside, for boat construction and maintenance, a saw mill, drying room, plus a large carpenters shop. The machinery throughout the depot was belt-driven from coal-fired steam engines, and this kept three stokers employed full time.

As a carpenter's apprentice, Colin worked with older, more experienced hands, such as Bill Aston and Wally Pope, men who were proud of their skills.

Colin recalls vividly that Bill in particular, was recognised, even by the rest of the men for being a highly skilled man, someone who could make any sort of object out of timber, and to a very high standard. As Colin learned the trade, men and apprentices would occasionally have a competitive but friendly race, to see who could produce a certain object first, and there was a great variety of items to choose from, including windows, doors, wheelbarrows and even ladders. Jack Jenkins, who was a little older than Colin, and remembers him starting, said that it was a pleasure to go to work at Ocker Hill and the men were proud of their skills.

Mr Banner, the general manager during the Second World War, at work in the engineering shop. Notice the old-fashioned collar and tie, plus bowler hat, which he always wore. He has a repaired, welded object, which looks like part of the extensive belt drive system that transferred power to the tools. The lathe shown had a 30ft bed and 5ft face plate. Much of the belting was leather, and the men were always keen to get their hands on it. Jack Jenkins told me that it was great for repairing your shoes.

Barrows, Boats & Caulking.

Three distinctly different wheelbarrows were fabricated at the yard, the largest of which was the mud barrow, used to transport the sludge away from the dredgers. These barrows were in constant use and were made of Ash with an Elm frame. In the saw mill, enormous balks of timber were converted to the required dimensions, while other planks were steamed in a long metal tank so that they could be bent and formed for the bows or stern of a boat (some boats were still made from timber even in the 1950s). Wooden boats were constructed with butted planks, this highly skilled work still left a tiny seam at the joint and these seams were made water tight by caulking with oakum, which was a common job on new and older craft. Oakum, a type of stranded hemp, was rolled into convenient lengths by the men using their fingers, usually across their thighs until it was the right thickness. Then the long strands of oakum were driven into the seams with large caulking mallets and chisels (the chisel blade was flat, like a bolster, but with a groove running along the edge). After all of the seams were thus treated, the exterior of the boat was given a thick coat of hot black tar using a Turk's head brush to complete the water proofing. Only then was the boat ready to be put into water.

Lock Gates & Calico (or chelico)

Lock gates, their pivots and waterway walls were continually in need of repair and maintenance and, on occasion, complete renewal of the gate was the only remedy. A lock gate weighing just over a ton may last, in theory, for 100 years. But on a busy section of canal, with continual opening and shutting, this could easily be reduced to around twenty years, and leaks soon appeared around the mating surfaces. Sometimes a refitting was sufficient, and a gang of men would be sent out to the job. After starting the day with the usual fry up and huge mug of tea, work would commence with the draining of a section of the canal. Sheer legs were erected over the gate if necessary to gently raise it from its hinge point. On light repairs damaged wood was chopped away with an adze, a tool used to face timber for thousands of years. Coming in different sizes and shaped like an axe with the blade set at right angles to the shaft, the adze was a well used tool. A sharp adze, in a skilled pair of hands was a superb instrument.

After chopping the damaged section away, a new piece of timber was measured, cut and fixed in position using chellico. This strange concoction was a mixture of tar and horse manure the latter being always readily available.

A metal pot was heated, and the manure was added to the tar until the experienced eye ascertained that the mixture was just right. This 'glue' then served as a sealant and bedding agent between old and new timber. The new timber was pushed into place, the chellico squeezed out and Colin remembers with great clarity that it was a good idea not to let chellico drop on your head if you happened to be working below.

Work in hand at Walsall Top Lock, 1934. Workmen here are using sheer legs to remove an old gate, ready for replacement. Though being used as a lifting device for thousands of years, sheer legs can be potentially dangerous, nowadays, a portable metal gantry is usually assembled and used. Notice the clothing of the day and the lockable wheelbarrow with all the necessary tools as well as the B.C.N. boat in the lock.

Jack Jenkins, born in 1929, started work at the B.C.N. maintenance depot at Ocker Hill, half way through the Second World War, at the age of fourteen. Mr Banner was still in charge, with Jack Barnet as the under manager. Workers at the depot included the two lock gate makers, Jack Aston and Harrold Abbots, and the blacksmith and his striker Teddy Davies and Harry Davies. One of the little oddities of Ocker Hill was that they always made the coffin for any employee who had worked there, and it was Sam Taylor the foreman who usually undertook this special assignment. The wood for coffins was stored under the floor until the sad event of an employee departing this earthly realm. In the timber mill were the two sawyers, Bill Homer and Harrold Davies. In the fitting shop was Wilfred Gill, Jack Philpot, Joe Wood, Frank Westwood, and Herbert Osbourn, (who was destined to be manager after Mr Banner) and often Jack James, when he wasn't tending the pump house at Titford (Oldbury). There were three painters and engine men, three stokers for the boilers, and Tom Bowen the electrician.

Jack was first assigned in 1943, to the iron boat dock. Here boats were drawn out of the water for repairs, especially hot riveting. Jack was taught to heat up rivets in a hearth and toss them to the workers in the boat. Every morning at 7.00 a.m., he would start work by going down to the Walsall canal to 'dip it'. This took place near the junction with the Tame Valley canal, where a metal plate was fitted to the waterway wall, where readings could be taken.

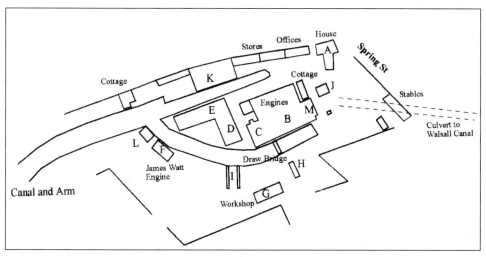

A. *Engineers House. B Boiler House. C. Carpenters Shop, though this was moved about 1950 to E.*
D. The Mill , where timbers were converted, using a large rack saw, lock gates were made in this area.
E. Fitting shop. F. The James Watt engine. G. Boat builders shop. H. Steaming tube for large planks.
I. Skids for lowering boats in to the water . J. Garage. K. Iron boat dock. L. On an old plan this is
marked as a Tar mill, but in later years it was the Yacht house where the Selene was kept. M. A weed
cutting boat was built in this area, and new welding techniques were practised.

After a year on the boat dock, Jack went into the fitting shop to broaden his practical education. These were the days before specialisation, and men tended to gain experience with more than one trade. Jack told me that after a man had been there some time, the gaffer would approach him and give him a job to get on with. If the task was accomplished successfully, you had a rise in your pay packet. Men worked inside and out of the depot, travelling with a bag of tools to locations around the B.C.N., you either went on your bicycle, or if the weather was foul, you went on the bus. In the depot, Jack spent time on the Lancashire boilers that supplied steam, and thus power, to the depot. There were six of these enormous cylindrical metal beasts, two to each steam engine. This meant one boiler could be taken out of operation for routine maintenance, or even a major overhaul, and the other boiler could keep the engine running. The men also went to the many pumping stations in the area to do repair jobs.

The war years saw a considerable rise in cigarette smoking, but there was still a demand for snuff, a finely ground blend of tobacco which had been used for well over a hundred years. Jack's boss, Mr Banner, was a regular snuff taker. He relates that Mr Banner (who everyone simply called 'Banner') would go up to him and say. 'Go and get me some snuff from Joss' (Joss Gittins was a shop at Ocker Hill island). He would then dispatch Jack with a shilling and when he returned with the S&P snuff wrapped in a little twist of paper, costing eleven pence and a halfpenny, Mr Banner would then, in the most generous manner, tell Jack to keep the halfpenny as though he were giving him a fortune.

After this tooing and fro-ing from Joss' had gone on for some time, Jack came across a small store of cayenne pepper at home that looked amazingly like snuff. He thought it would be fun to mix it with Mr Banner's next quarter of an ounce. He bided his time until the occasion presented itself and carefully mixed a pinch of the pepper into the snuff. Jack reckons that the ensuing sneezes could be heard as far away as Wednesbury! Mr Banner gave Jack one of his withering looks across the top of his spectacles, and never sent him for snuff again.

Two years after the end of the last war, young men in Britain were still being called up for their two years compulsory service in the armed forces. Jack went into the army, did his bit and came out in 1950. His first job was on a milk round in the Ocker Hill area. One day as he was passing the repair yard, Mr Osbourne, who had now taken over as manager, saw Jack and called him over. 'Never mind that' he said, referring to the milk cart. 'I've got a job for you here, and there's a house going at Bloomfield'. And so it was that Jack ended up back at the Ocker Hill depot. 1950 was a good year for Jack in many ways as it turned out. He had come out of the army, got his old job back, got married, and moved into what was an extremely desirable residence.

The well riveted boat L.F.S. 21(London Fire service) was a smoke boat in the Second World War. Their job was to flood smoke onto the rivers and canals around the capital, thus obscuring the glittering water from the German aircraft. After parts of an Ice boat was married in to it, it became the tug Tardebigge.

A shot from inside the L.F.S. boat above. Bolted to the floor near the door is the steam winch that was used to haul boats out of the arm and into the repair room. The boats were guided out of the canal onto and along a small rail system equipped with bogies, and one of them can be seen in front of the winch.

One of the pleasure craft being constructed by British Waterways during the late 1950s, before the Ocker Hill depot was shut down and sold off. Colin Williams is on the left, and Bill Aston on the right.

One of those early return to work tasks, was to effect some repair work at the pumping station over at Bradley. The land adjacent to this pump was in a few years to become the new British Waterways Depot that was destined to take over all the work from Ocker Hill.

The pumping engine was sited at the side of the old 1772 Bradley loop. The original engine had been the beam type, set to pump water out of 'Iron Mad' Wilkinson's mines and into the canal. The old atmospheric engine had long been replaced in 1935 by a Sulzer. This shaft-driven impeller unit, was itself to be exchanged for three submersible pumps in 1956.

In the late 1950s, the Ocker Hill depot was coming to the end of an eventful and busy existence that had begun just after the first Birmingham canal of 1772 was opened. The British Waterways fleet was essentially being broken up, and they were testing the new waters of the leisure trade, building boats for pleasure and accommodation, often from existing hulls. Old trades were disappearing and new ideas embraced. Rivets were being replaced by electrical welding, and modern glues taking the place of chellico. In 1961, after 187 long years of maintaining the B.C.N., the Ocker Hill depot closed its gates for the last time.

B.C.N. Houses

The B.C.N., and later British Waterways, owned a considerable amount of property, including depots, warehouses, stables and workers houses. Colin was born and raised in a typical example. The house, one of two pairs, stood half way down the Ryders Green flight (8 locks) on the Walsall canal as it comes into Great Bridge, Tipton. Most of those well-built houses have been demolished, but some examples can still be found near the Tividale aqueduct.

Just a few yards along the towpath was a minor depot, consisting of blacksmith's shop and carpenters work room. The B.C.N. houses at Ryders Green locks were a good sized semi, with three upstairs rooms, and the complete house was adequately lit by large attractive paraffin lamps, that were suspended from the centre of the ceilings by lengths of adjustable chain. Downstairs there were two rooms, a kitchen with a coal-fired boiler, and a verandah. Food was kept in the pantry, and to help keep certain items cool (no fridges in those days) they were placed on a settlas, essentially a thick marble slab. Few houses were equipped with flushing toilets during the 1950s. Outside, a few yards from the house was a small brick building fitted inside with a low brick chamber to receive the 'soil'. The seating arrangements consisted of wooden boards with suitable holes. This little room was known nationally as 'The Privvy'. At regular intervals the 'Night Soil' men, working for the local council, came in their trucks and shovelled everything away.

A spoon dredger, operating close to the wharf of Noah Hingley's (Netherton). Canal beds soon filled up with silt and other rubbish, causing boats to sometimes get stuck fast on the bottom, and the spoon dredger was the only answer to this problem until mechanised dredgers came along.

The Ice Breakers

An extremely hazardous task on all canals during those cold winter months was clearing ice from the canal's surface, thus maintaining traffic flow. No work in those days meant no wages, and lengthy stoppages caused hardship for all concerned. Stoppages due to ice were an enormous disadvantage to the canal system and ultimately a major nail in its coffin.

At the Ocker Hill depot, there were two ice-breaking boats on hand for this purpose. The ice-breakers were designed specifically for that work, and were unlike any other boats on the system. About half the length of a regular narrow boat, they had a rounded hull section and a sharp prow. The boats could have been wood or metal construction, but the wooden hulls were clad in sheet metal to give them added protection. Five or more horses could be attached to the boat to provide the power and speed that was necessary to break up the ice, and the men controlling the horses often had to follow at a trot. A team of around eight men dressed for the weather with thick overcoats, would board the boat, arranging themselves into two rows down the centre line of the craft. As the boat went along, at around five to eight miles per hour, they would hang on to a thick central rope, fastened to two short masts, and rock the boat from side to side, thus breaking up the ice. This all sounds like a crazy operation, but in truth, great experience and skill was required to perform this fast and dangerous operation, especially during the dark hours, as horses and men could easily slip into the water with disastrous consequences.

The Spoon Dredger

The usual three man crew are seen in the photograph opposite, operating the spoon dredger. On the right of the men is the windlass that dragged the spoon along the bed of the canal, while the man second from right is operating the small crane that lifted the heavy spoon up from the murky depths, with its heavy wet load (there were holes in the spoon to allow excess water to drain away). The man to the left with the brimmed hat, has hold of the end of the shaft connected to the spoon itself.

This was a hard manual job for all three men, as was emptying the load and barrowing the sludge away at the end of the day. Dredging was therefore a laborious task and several crews and their boats were employed throughout the Midlands on this vital task of keeping the waterways free. Jack Garrett from Tipton like so many others spent much of his working life on these boats, and Jack recalls working at this particular site at Hingley's, Netherton, being paid about £12 per week in the 1950s for it.

Great Bridge

The map on page 54 of the Great Bridge area (Tipton), is an extract from the 1921 Ordnance Survey, produced at 6in to the mile, though our example has been greatly reduced. The distance from Great Bridge to the railway at Dudley Port is more or less one mile.

It is amazing to see how much of the Black Country's canal and industrial system, with its progressive development, has been crammed into two square miles. The Walsall canal opened in June 1799. It enters the frame half way down the right hand edge, comes into Great Bridge and heads N.W. toward Toll End. The Haines branch comes off that, at a junction by the railway interchange basin, going southwest to a dead end by the Pump House brick works. In the far left corner is the Birmingham-Wolverhampton Main Line (Telford's 1830s). In the top left corner we can see some of the Toll End communication canal and its locks. This is one of the earliest arms, coming from the Old Main line near Tipton and serving Horseley Heath with its collieries and Iron Works.

A later canal, the Dixon's Branch, ran parallel with the one just mentioned, from the new line to where Horseley later built their engineering works. Collieries also abound on this small map, and there are at least five places of coal extraction marked. Add to that the total of four brick works, plus two iron works, *all* having important links with the canal network. Note also the well established rail network that came in the late nineteenthth century, and the rail/canal interchange basin (by the 'G' in Great Bridge) showing the close relationship that grew between these two totally different modes of transport. The one here at Great Bridge was one of over thirty throughout the B.C.N.

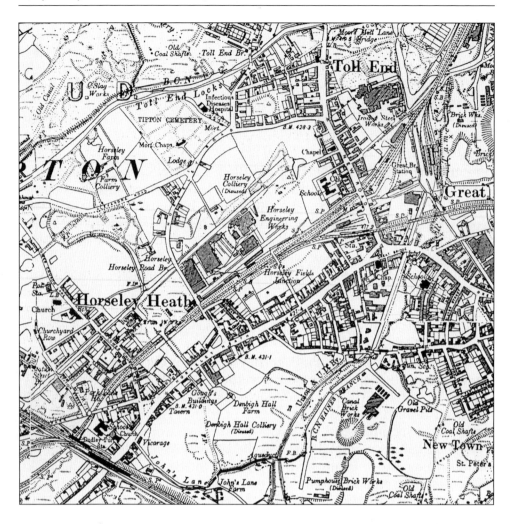

Horsley & Toll End Bridges

The early Horseley Coal & Iron Works, was where the Great Bridge map shows 'slag works' and 'old coal shafts', Horsley's later engineering works, and Toll End Iron Works are less than a mile apart, yet they represent only a fraction of the iron production for the immediate area. Our interest however lies in the fact that between them, they are responsible for some of the most attractive and durable canal bridges in England. I must add at this point that Horseley designed much larger bridges than these relatively and they went to many parts of the globe

Let us now however go back to our Toll End Branch to see how it developed along with the birth of the Horseley Works. In 1783 the Birmingham Canal company sought, and obtained the power to extend a branch from Tipton to serve the mines that were being dug between Tipton and Toll End. The company was at this stage known as the Horseley Coal Co., and they had not as yet branched into the iron industry. The drawing below shows this arm, basins & pools, some time later around 1857. Horseley's attention by then had switched from coal extraction to iron production.

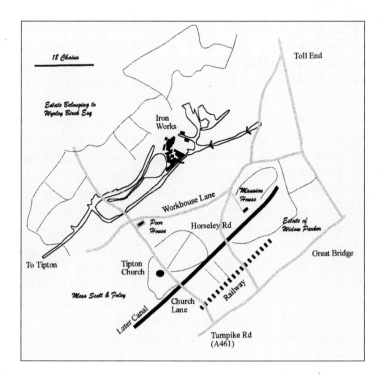

So at the outset, the canal company decided to *'level and make an estimate of executing the same, both with and without locks, and to stake out such a branch in the line which will be most commodious to the mine and land owner'*. The original partnership proposed that the branch be built with two locks, but one week later they realised that three would be necessary to cope with the 15ft rise of the land.

The canal company agreed to pay half the cost of the locks, stipulating that the locks should not be damaged by the mine workings. Work went ahead on a branch with three locks, with a rise of 5ft at each one. £84 got the ball rolling and the canal was to be completed in two stages. The initial work was to be completed by 1793. Things started well, but two years later complaints started to come in to the canal company that the headroom of one of the bridges was so low, that it prevented access by some of the taller Oxfordshire cabins.

The bridge was raised and more wharves were added. Joseph Amphlett, one of the three partners of the Horseley Coal Co., took up residence in a fine house marked on an early map near Horsley Heath simply as 'The Mansion'. This same house was described in 1798 by 'Shaw' as 'An excellent square house, pleasantly situated at a proper distance from the coal works'. Interestingly some two miles away in West Bromwich, the Earl of Dartmouth moved away from his 'excellent residence' because this distance became a touch too close.

Hickmans Iron Works, Bilston. This photo perfectly shows the relationship and dependency of the canal/iron works to each other. At least seven boats full of coal are waiting to be unloaded at the sheds. This was extremely hard work, but at least there was some shelter from the elements. On the left, iron is being loaded onto more boats to be shipped away.

In 1797, a Mr Robins, working for the canal company, made a survey of the land regarding this branch and its locks. The assessed cost of the work was £1,369, 5s 3d. And so the Horseley Company started its mining operations with three shafts, two of those equipped with a 'whimsey' (horse-operated winding gear) and the other having a pumping engine. However, as more shafts were dug, ground movement started to have an effect on the canal bed and its locks. This was to become a huge problem not only for this branch, but for much of the Black Country in the years to come, as shafts and tunnels riddled the subterranean depths.

In 1802 the middle lock cracked, and two years later one lock had sunk by a foot (300mm). Estimates were given that the locks were in danger of sinking by four to five feet! This was also about the time that Horseley were to move from the coal business to iron, a decision that was to bring to the canals of Britain, bridges of great character and, dare I say it, even an art form. Many of these lovely bridges exhibit a combination of elegance, coupled with simplicity of design. They incorporate sweeping curves and straight lines, diamond and box shapes, to create an extremely strong structure that has withstood the test of time and heavy usage. A variety of patterned, iron castings were made for bridge sides. In effect each 'side' of the bridge constituted the support for the decking and the hand or guard rail, was either one, two or three castings.

After being transported to the site, the sides were lowered onto the finished stone or brick abutments, with their curved wing walls. Then the cast, flanged, oblong decking plates were bolted between them. After the decking had received its surface, the bridge was ready for use. The cost? About £140 each.

Between 1820 and 1858, Horseley and Toll End Iron Works were responsible for creating some of the loveliest bridges throughout Britain's inland waterway network.

Aston Junction, Birmingham, with its Horseley Bridge

A detail of the 1829 bridge, at Bromford Junction.

A one off – the little cantilever foot bridge at the bottom of Factory Locks, Tipton.

The oldest Horsley canal bridge I know of, is about a mile from Brentford, known as Gallows Bridge, and is stamped 1820. Also uniquely it has the canal company's name stamped there as well 'Grand Junction Canal Company'. However, many fine examples can be found right here in the Black Country. I am most fortunate in having two examples close at hand. Both display different styles, with nineteen years between them. They are a short distance from my home in West Bromwich at Bromford Junction, though I must say that the earlier example has the more attractive casting.

The largest, finest and most famous of the canal bridges must be the 1829 Galton bridge in Smethwick. Telford may not have designed it, but he must have had a say in its construction. The Galton bridge (named after Samuel Galton, the Quaker and gunsmith) spans the deep cutting at Smethwick. This magnificent bridge has a single span of 150ft, and a height of 70ft above the waters surface, vaulted the biggest man made earthworks of its day.

Now only a footbridge, it can be easily accessed from Smethwick High St, next to the station. Its eastern prospect has been lost to some extent due to the addition of a new road tunnel, but a good view can still be had from this point. The design of the bridge is far removed from its simpler relatives, and close observation shows many castings, bolted together in six interconnected ribs.

It was the Galton bridge that formed part of the great improvements between 1827 and 1830 on the main Wolverhampton to Birmingham line. The smallest Horseley bridge I know of, is the little cantilever bridge that sits over the tail of the third lock at Factory locks, Tipton. With its tiny span of around seven feet, and gap for towrope, it is a delight for walkers to use.

Both of Horseley's sites have been built over, and only the bridges it produced stand as silent memorials to an industrial era that spanned 200 years, and filled the lives of many local folk.

A Horseley Bridge gracefully decorates a re-developed Birmingham at Old Turn Junction.

The Galton Bridge Smethwick. Another very attractive bridge/aqueduct, is the engine arm aqueduct that takes the canal over the new main line, also at Smethwick. Sporting a most unusual Gothic pointed arch design, this work of art wouldn't look out of place in a church. Although this structure is credited to Horseley by other historians, there is no maker's stamp to prove its pedigree.

A Bridge Spotting List

Below is a list of all the Horseley and Toll End canal bridges I know of, perhaps you may know of another one?

HORSELEY

Galton Bridge	Smethwick	1829
Factory locks	Tipton	*c.*1827
Delph locks	Brierley Hill	1858
Albion Junction	West Bromwich	
Bromford Junction	West Bromwich	
2 bridges, 2 styles from 1829 & 1848		
Smethwick Junction	2 bridges	1828
Winson Green		1848
Aston Top Lock	Birmingham	1828
Nile st	Birmingham	1827
Old Turn Junction	Birmingham	1827
Gallows Bridge	Brentford	1820

TOLL END

Netherton Junction, two bridges
Windmill End, Netherton, three bridges.

Oxford Canal, 1831-33

Bridge No.8 (moved to Coventry 1969)
No.32 Brinklow Arm
No.39 All Oaks lane
No.45 Newbold Arm
No.53 Rugby Wharf Arm
No.93 Barlows dock entrance, now a marina.
Plus a double span bridge at Braunston Turn

For three of these bridges on the Oxford, Horseley were paid £419 12s 10d in October 1832, and £693 for the remaining five in January 1833.

Burst at Dudley Port. 9th Sept. 1899.

The enormous devastation here ably demonstrates what can happen when a canal breaks its banks, and several miles of canal quickly empty themselves. Fortunately no one was killed in this particular incident, but at least one boat was dragged away. The scene is September 1899 at Dudley Port, close to the Netherton Junction (Tipton). This section of canal was part of Telford's improvements of the 1830s, and rides high on a long embankment. Telford couldn't foresee however that the close workings of the Rattlechain Brickwork's would seriously undermine his otherwise substantial and laudable earthworks.

This contrasting shot shows a large group of people, obviously dressed in their best attire, taking it easy on a day out. Large cushions have been placed at the front of the boat for complete relaxation for the ladies. The narrowboat Hector *is from Oldbury, and the date is around the turn of the twentieth century. The location could be Titford pools, as they are on an apparently wide stretch of water, but this is by no means certain.*

Tipton and its Canals

Tip,n ON Cut is how many of the locals refer to their hometown and it's easy to see why. The photograph on the next page, taken around 1960, shows Tipton before it was changed. Taken from the 'Beehive' bridge, we are looking away from the junction with the old main line canal, and across the first three locks of the Tipton Green and Toll End Communication Canal. Built to serve the original Horseley Works as an arm. It became a through canal when it was connected to the Walsall canal. It was just under two miles long with ten locks.

When Telford's Island line was built, along with the three Factory locks, a four way junction was produced. Notice how sharp the original canal bend was at the Malt House, before the New Line joined it and produced a new junction. In later years when the eastern end of the Toll End canal was lost, the basin by the junction came to be used by 'Caggy Stevens,' one of the last horse boaters on the system. Close to what was Tipton Green junction is the 'Fountain', a pub run in the nineteenth century by William Perry who became known as the Tipton Slasher. William in his younger years worked on the canals and it is reported that he learned his pugilistic skills, fighting with other boatmen over lock disputes.

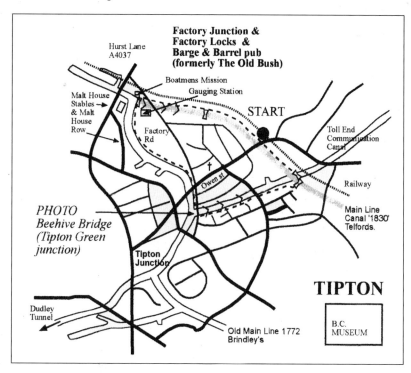

63

Discovering Tipton, a circular walk taking just over an hour.

The trail can be started at many points, but the Tipton rail station seems a logical point for me to commence my narrative.

With the rail station on your right, access can be gained straight on to the towpath. We are now on the New Main Line, part of Thomas Telford's improvements of the late 1820s. The first towpath bridge is known as Three Furnaces Bridge, and underneath it ran a short arm into the Tipton Green Furnace Co., the last blast furnace plant in Tipton. This site is now occupied by the rail station. Continue along the towpath toward Factory locks. Running parallel with the canal on the opposite side is Brick Kiln St.

The bottom lock soon comes into view after passing Wood St footbridge. The locks take boats from the Birmingham level '453ft' up to the Wolverhampton 473ft level, using three chambers. Don't miss the unique cantilever footbridge, cast by Horseley. The gap on the one side was to allow the towrope to pass.

Tipton - The only town to have its High Street totally encircled by canals.
Almost everything here has gone, except the flats in the distance. A walkway has recently been made along the line of the canal, and remains of the second lock can still be found as a feature. The bridge in the distance is the Globe Bridge, while the chimney stack belonged to Chatwyns Foundry. With a magnifying glass it is just possible to make out the name of the terraced house on the right, Horse Shoe Row. The street parallel with the locks to the North was 'Canal Street', would you believe?

Horseley bridge at Pelsall, this time a unique combination of iron and brick.

To the right of bottom lock, was Bullers Engineering, and a nearby slag wall was made from the waste material of the metal processing that took place here. Factory Road bridge, crosses the canal between the first and second lock. Built with extremely strong blue bricks, some are stamped with the name 'Whitehouse Bloomfield' and the firm of Whitehouse, one of many brick making establishments in Tipton, was close at hand.

Standing on the other side of Top Lock is the Tipton Gauging Station, covered a few pages on in the book. The station at its height could deal with two boats at a time, and in the end wall, it is possible to see the date of construction (1873), and the two arched entrance ways (now bricked up). Between 1873 and 1900 the station saw over 10,000 boats registered.

Just a few yards down from the Gauging Station, to the right of the towpath, is a building now occupied by a roofing firm, but in times past this was a small place of worship. This particular 'Boatmen's Mission' was one of five originally built around the B.C.N. of which two still survive with the other at Birchills (Walsall) being part of the small museum there. The one at Tipton was largely funded by the Earl of Dudley, costing around £1,000 to construct. Its purpose was to bring a little comfort to the boatmen who passed. Light refreshments could be taken inside.

Services were held on Sundays in the mission and surrounding wharves, in the hope of bringing spiritual enlightenment to the boatmen and their families, and maybe lure them away from the pubs for a while. The bell tower has gone but the building still has its foundation stone with the words 'To The Glory Of God And for the Good of the Souls of Those Who Pass on the Canal'.

A perfectly matching pair of Toll End bridges at Netherton Junction, Dudley Port, Tipton.

Factory bridge is in front of us. The Barge and Barrel pub sits revamped on our right. Perhaps someone should tell the necessary bodies, that the nearest place for barges is Stourport, some twenty miles away, still we know what they mean. Factory junction takes its name from the nearby factory belonging in the early nineteenth century to Mr James Keir (1735-1820). The factory's site is now occupied by a more modern industrial estate just under the bridge.

Mr Keir (a Scot) lived in a variety of places in the Black Country, but mostly at Hill Top, West Bromwich. From his factory in Tipton he gained a reputation as a contributor to science and industry. After working in the glass making industry near Stourbridge, he came to Tipton in 1780, a few years after the construction of the canal, to produce alkali at Bloomfield. The Tipton works in time came to be almost wholly concerned with the soap manufacture, but Keir also manufactured his own metallic alloy, known as Keir's metal.

This Tipton factory came to be regarded in its time as a technological marvel, being powered by steam and water. The factory used about nine tons of coal a day, so Keir, along with a partner, sank a mine in Tividale (about two miles along the canal) and there is still a bridge with his name, in that area. Factory junction only became so, after the construction of the Telford line, before that it was simply a sharp bend in the Wolverhampton-Birmingham canal, as it turned right toward the Rowley hills, taking advantage of the contour lines.

Gauging Stations

Canal companies earned their money by charging fees from the boats that passed their toll stations (which were scattered around the B.C.N.). The gauging stationis still extant but hasn't been used for the purpose of gauging boats for some years and has until recently been used as a factory unit. Built in 1873, the depot is a long, blue brick structure. It was capable of taking two boats at a time into its parallel basins. The basins were connected to the canal, by a short arm, just above the lock. Boats entered through two semi-circular portals, both of which have been bricked up, but they can be clearly seen from the towpath opposite.

The sketch depicts gauging in the 1950s, when the station was only in use one day a week. Fred Heritage is the man in the boat with his back to us. He is guiding one of the one ton weights, operated by a steam powered unit, into position. Leaning on the boat is Arthur Williams (Colin's father) who was lock keeper at Ryders Green. In the background is Leonard, the clerk who oversaw the operation and recorded the details. A fourth person operated the boiler.

One ton weights were lowered into position along the length of the boat, and readings were taken from four points. The gauges can be seen attached to the gunwales. Readings continued to be taken as the weight was gradually increased. This work was undertaken on all new boats, and any that had major repairs or alterations.

Tipton Gauging Station, as it appears today.

A Bit Of The Black Country. A narrow boat family, with their boat and horse at Union St, Tipton. The boat belongs to the Shropshire Union Canal Carrying Company. Notice the wooden crates and barrels

At the junction we cross over the footbridge to follow the original 1772 route, while on the right, are the Malthouse stables. The stables, built in 1845, were to accommodate the many horses that hauled the boats past this point and there were fourteen cobbled stalls on the lower floor. The upper storey was for fodder and storage. The building has been carefully renovated and turned into a leisure centre, but still retains the arched windows with cast iron frames. The stables were used as such until the 1920s.

The canal and towpath now start a long sweeping curve to the left, before an even sharper right hand turn, taking it under Owen Street Bridge. The curved wall is still much the same as it was, when the boatman and his family (on page 66) sat upon it. By the bridge is the Fountain Inn, one of Tipton's oldest pubs, where for a period during the nineteenth century, it was inhabited by one of the town's most famous persons, known as, 'The Tipton Slasher'. William Perry, born near the canal in 1819, became a boatman like his father. During the early 19th century the local canals were very busy affairs, with boats regularly having to wait in queues to go through locks.

This waiting caused a great deal of frustration, and fights often broke out, as boatmen attempted to jump the queue. It was this early rough and tumble, that served William well as an apprenticeship for his later boxing career. He became the bare knuckle prize fighting champion of England from 1850 to 1857, and is portrayed on the pub sign, and on a plaque near the entrance.

Coronation Gardens is now a pleasantly landscaped area, but in past times was a coal wharf, and later a malt house. In the far distance is Dudley Castle, the real seat of power from before Norman times until the Elizabethan age. The early fortifications were timber, but from the 1300s onwards it was rebuilt as a stone castle, and developed for the next 200 years. During the Civil War it was held by the Royalists, while the Parliamentarians bombarded it from the hill opposite. A small skirmish between opposing forces took place about 200yards away in 1644, becoming known as 'The Battle of Tipton Green'. Coronation gardens sits opposite the junction of what was the Tipton and Toll End Communication Canal . From here, a newish walkway follows the line of the old canal parallel with Owen Street and you will come across the remains of the second lock mentioned earlier. After Union Street there was first, the Patent Borax Co., followed by Chatwins Foundry.

This takes us back to the main line canal, which was at one time a busy four way junction. The small basin at the left of the junction was formerly occupied by a railway interchange basin (later Caggy Stevens boatyard). It is now only a short walk back to our start point at Tipton railway station. Notice the weather vane that commemorates the worlds first iron steam ship *Aaron Manby* built at the Horseley Iron Works.

An extremely busy boating scene at Factory Junction, Bloomfields, in the early twentieth century. The Malt house stables is on the right. More than a dozen narrow boats are moored here opposite the boatmans Mission. In the distance is Elwells coal yard on Malthouse Row, just one of the many coal merchants in this area. Elwells was a typical coal wharf, recieving coal direct from the colleries to be distributed locally. An office and stores were located off the yard where hay and corn were kept for their horses. Jack Garret lived in Malthouse Row during the 1930s and his father worked for Alfred Matty, a small canal carrying company.

Smethwick Locks. A fine view of the old and new main line. This photograph was taken while the toll house was still standing. The two lines of locks on the old line were built to ease congestion, but the one on the left has long gone, as has the brass foundry that gave the name to Brasshouse Lane.

Samuel Barlow & Canal Carrying Co.

In the 1940s, Joseph Garrett worked as a skipper for Samuel Barlow & Canal Carrying Co., mainly from their Glascote base near Tamworth, but occasionally from other locations. Barlow's were a sizeable firm at this time and had a busy depot at Braunston on the Grand Union. The wharf Joseph was most familiar with was this one, on the Coventry canal in Glascote, at 41 John St. The main offices for Barlow's were in Birmingham city centre, at the Exchange Buildings.

Joseph's son, Philip, worked with his father from the age of fourteen, as soon as he left school, serving as mate for the next four years, Philip fondly remembers those days. In the 1940s Barlow's had, at Tamworth, about eight skippers working such boats as the *Teddy*, *Stanley*, *Rose of Sharron*, *Joyce*, *Josephine* or *Margaret*. The bulk of trade in this area was concentrated on the movement of coal from pits like Baddesley to supply the Coventry and Nechells power stations.

A typical week's work for Joseph and Phil started on Monday morning at the early hour of 5.15a.m., and they would prepare to take a pre-loaded boat up the canal toward Birmingham. Phil uses the term 'up to Brum' even though going south, because the locks through Curdworth, Minworth and Salford, and of course the '21' were all uphill.

From Smethwick junction, they took the right fork onto the Old Main line, and up the three Smethwick locks to their destination at Kenricks of West Bromwich. Joseph and Phil did not unload the boat at this point, but instead they transferred the tiller, helm, mast and bottle stove (there were three sizes of these) and their personal possessions from the boat they had just brought in, onto an empty one. These items, if left on a boat, could easily be stolen or damaged. They would then bring the empty boat back to Glascote for loading, a journey of two days. On Wednesday they would, more often than not, repeat the same run.

Things were a little more exciting in the winter months, when Barlow's had the contract from the B.C.N. to keep the canals open by doing the ice breaking. This was on the Birmingham Fazeley canal and five miles of the Coventry canal, which the B.C.N. had oversight of. So, when conditions were bad and the canal started to freeze over, an icebreaker started out from the Fazeley end, working its way south toward Salford until it met another ice boat working north from Gravelly. The winters of 1946 and 1947 were particularly bad and both boats and men were laid up for long periods. As a result the canals started to lose the trade that they had enjoyed for many years. Another factor was the increased use of the ten-ton truck, which could operate in all weather, and was obviously faster. Barlow's were sensible enough however to start using these vehicles themselves. Many of these trucks bought by independent operators were ex-army surplus.

By the 1950s Barlow's as a canal carrying concern was virtually finished, and when Phil came out of the army after his two year stint, he found F.M.C. and the Grand Union Canal Carrying Co., all under the banner of British Waterways, and their early, rather uninspiring, blue and yellow paint scheme.

The Canal Boats Act. 1877.

Every boat with a cabin from this date forward was required to carry a document called the *Certificate of Registration of Canal Boat.* Issued by the local council, it provided the basis for local officials to make spot checks on individual boats at any location, to make sure that they were of a reasonable standard for human habitation. Joseph's document for the boat *Kingswood* is shown. It was kept safe in a brown envelope, and was usually found in the ticket draw at the rear of the cabin for quick reference. Essentially it contained brief information of the boat, the owner, how many persons the cabin could be used for and their sleeping conditions, and the three main points are interesting enough to reprint.

This document, issued by Tamworth District Council Registration Authority, was then signed by Joseph Garrett.

(a) Subject to the conditions herein-after prescribed, with respect to the separation of the sexes, the number of persons who may be allowed to dwell in the boat shall be such that in the cabin or cabins of the boat there shall not be less than 60 cubic feet of free air space for each person above the age of 12 years, and not less than 40 cubic feet of free air space for each child under the age of 12 years.

Provided that in the case of a boat built prior to the Thirtieth day of June , One thousand eight hundred and seventy eight, the free air space for each child under the age of 12 years shall be deemed sufficient if it is not less than 30cubic feet.

Provided also, that in the case of a boat registered as a 'fly' boat and worked by shifts, by four persons above the age of 12 years, there shall be not less than, 180 cubic feet of free air space in any cabin occupied as a sleeping place by any two of such persons at on and the same time.

(b) A cabin occupied as a sleeping place by a husband and wife shall not, at any time while in such occupation, be occupied as a sleeping place by any other person of the female sex above the age of 12 years, or by any other person of the male sex above the age of 14 years.

Provided that in the case of a boat built prior to the Thirtieth day of June,

One thousand eight hundred and seventy eight, a cabin occupied as a sleeping place by a husband and wife may be occupied by one other person of the male sex above the age of 14 years, subject to the following conditions-
  i That the cabin be not occupied as a sleeping place by any other person than those above mentioned .
  ii That the part of the cabin which may be used as a sleeping place by the husband and wife shall, at all times, while in actual use, be effectually separated from the part used as a sleeping place by the other occupant of the cabin by means of a sliding or otherwise movable screen or partition of wood or other solid material, so constructed or placed as to provide for efficient ventilation.

(c) A cabin occupied as a sleeping place by a person of the male sex above the age of 14 years shall not, at any time, be occupied as a sleeping place by a person of the female sex above the age of 12 years, unless she be the wife of the male occupant, or of one of the male occupants in any case within the proviso to rule (b).

Right: One of James Dudfields boats, Dove, comfortably moored on the river Severn. Men and boys are seen here at the turn of the twentieth century, taking a well deserved break after loading hay for the Cannock pit ponies. Notice on the side of the boat, the registration number, plus the B.C.N. number for use at the gauging stops.

Left: A B.C.N. Boundary post. Which has of recent years given its title to the B.C.N.S. magazine.

Stourport and its Basins, Past and Present

To really make the most of what Stourport has to offer, take a leisurely stroll around the canal basins. The constant changing levels make this a fascinating area to explore. Then watch the action in the locks, as boat after boat makes its entrance from the turbulent waters of the river Severn. A good place to start is at the Tontine Hotel, from here you can cross at the wide locks, and walk along the river toward the narrow staircase locks. Turn right here, along the locks, past the dry dock on your left, and over the swivel bridge. Bridge numbers are shown, except No.3 which was lost in a development of the area. Then continue along Engine Lane, down to the bridge over the top barge lock. From here you can walk around the Chandlery (A) then return to the Tontine for a drink, and watch the world go by.

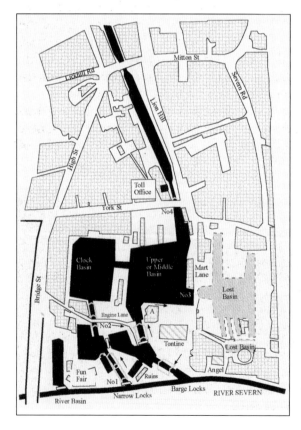

The map clearly shows the canal entering from the north end of town, through York Lock, and into the first of several basins. After the canal opened in 1772 the quiet little hamlet of Lower Mitton became Stourport. Instantly quays and warehouses started to appear, along with the masts of the elegant Severn trows. In 1776 the designer and writer John Nash came to visit this thriving new port and had this to say 'where once stood an alehouse, Brindley has caused a town to be erected. Made a port and dockyards, built a new and elegant bridge to span the river, established markets and made this Maritime town in the heart of England not only the wonder of the county but of the nation too.'

The furthermost basin, seen above, has long gone, as has bridge No.3 that was the entrance into this basin, with its dry docks and black sheds. Coal from Ashwood was unloaded by electric grabs, and conveyed straight to the power station only a few hundred yards away. When the power station's life came to an end, so did this basin. It was filled in and became a timber yard for some years. The other lost basin was also filled in and became the site of a former Gas Works. A basin was lost, and so too was a reservoir of water for the locks. On busy boating days the water level in the remaining basins can drop considerably.

Four locks raise boats from the river into the top basin (sometimes called the middle basin). The lower two have a rise of 11ft 10in, while the upper two have a rise of 13ft. The Middle basin is the oldest, being built at the same time as the canal. The basin to its left is now known as the 'clock basin', from the clock on an old warehouse, now the headquarters of the Stourport Yacht Club.

Phil Garrett became basin attendant at Stourport from 1974. He has had many happy, busy years, giving advice and selling useful items to boaters, new and old and issuing licences. On occasion he also recalls the gruesome side of the job when witnessing bodies being pulled out of the river and locks.

Stourport's lost warehouses. A hive of activity in days past.

Stourport, at the bottom of the barge locks. The two boats seen here in the late 1950s are part of British Waterways Northern Fleet, and have come out of the wide lock together. In the distance is the power station built in 1926. Its thirst for coal was to dominate the lives of many a boat crew for the next fifty years. In front of the station is Holbrooks vinegar factory, and I well remember the unmistakable smell when I went there on holidays as a lad in the 1960s and fished from the bank opposite.

The view under Mart Lane bridge (as was) from the lost basin toward the upper or middle basin.

Maintenance, On and Around the B.C.N.

As soon as the major construction of the Birmingham Canal Navigation was finished, the work of maintaining it began. Looking after the almost 160 miles of canal, with its locks, pounds, bridges and towpaths, was an enormous task, and several depots, with their trained men and apprentices, were kept gainfully employed. Depots such as Ocker Hill, Icknield Port and Sneyd had their own individual teams of brickies, carpenters and fitters who travelled about the system to effect the repairs, and George Smith came to be among that number.

George was born in 1927 into a Birmingham that has long disappeared. The house he first lived in was at Cambrian Wharf, opposite the Crescent. Behind the Crescent was the old Bingley Hall, while along the canal at the junction (Old Turn) was the Malthouse and sidings, a complex rail terminus. His father, Thomas Henry Smith, was a 'carter', driving a horse and cart for Picktons, who collected parcels from around the town for delivery further afield. In 1942 the family moved into a B.C.N. house right in Gas Street basin. The number was 34 and it still survives, but has now been converted into the 'Tap and Spile' pub. George's father, after carting, went to work for the canal company on its boats. In time George made his start too but as a mate to the bricklayers.

Working in gangs of four, composed of two brickies and their mates, they were sent anywhere on the system. Starting work at 7 a.m., they used a horse-drawn boat containing their tools and building materials, as base of operations. There was also a small winch on the boat to cope with heavy lifting work.

The house on Gas Street was well made and had seven rooms, making it a comfortable residence. The house, like the basin, was supplied with gas lighting from the gas works a few yards distant. The gas was piped around the house and to lamps in the centre of the ceiling, which were operated by chains that turned a tap on the lamp assembly. The lamp in the living room had three mantles to supply extra light. Mantles were a soft cloth gauze that fitted over the gas burner. When lit, the gauze glowed with amazing heat and light. The gauzes once used were extremely fragile and if knocked simply disintegrated. The lamps had glass balls over them, which also need to be treated with care.

During those years, George's father was operating one of the horse-drawn boats on short runs, which included coal transport from Hamstead Basin to Ocker Hill Depot. The depot ran all its machinery by steam, generated from a large boiler room that was constantly busy, and therefore required a regular supply of coal. George recalls that this day boat was kept at Icknield Port depot, and the horse they used was named 'Dolly'.

Dolly was a short dappled grey at 10½ hands, but she pulled well and George was fond of her pleasant temperament. After working some time with the building team he went to work with his father, and they took it in turns to steer the boat or walk the horse. It was soon clear that George and his dad couldn't get on. 'He always had to have things his own way' was George's remark.

'Even as I grew older my parents were always very strict. When I was younger, and we lived at Cambrian Wharf, I remember being very friendly with some of the children that lived on the boats. My father was not always keen on me playing with them, but one day I sneaked onto the wharf to see my best friend. When the old lock keeper caught me there, he sent me away with a clout round the ear. On arriving home I received another one from my dad.

'In 1948 we swapped over from a horse boat to a diesel tug, and I know that my dad wasn't pleased with the change at all. He lamented the loss of his horse, and said that working the boat was now much harder, especially at locks when you were towing a butty.'

George is certain that all the horses on the canal were ex-London, Midland & Scottish (LMS) horses, and had been employed on railways. Behind where the Indoor Arena is today, there was an enormous goods yard, where many horses were used to shunt rail trucks around. The horseshoe stables, a remarkable bit of circular brickwork, that still exists, was built for them, not the canal horses.

Hamstead Stop Island, near Gorse Farm, Perry Bar, during a stoppage in 1936. Hamstead Colliery basin is behind to the right. The seven men here are repairing a bulge that developed in the waterway wall. The masonry has deteriorated to such an extent, from use and erosion, that a large section was in danger of collapse.

Stop planks have been placed to the right of the island, a gate with paddle gear has closed off the other side. On the island itself a large heavy Ceres pump is drawing out the remaining water and sludge into the adjoining pound. The pumps were kept and maintained at Ocker hill. The work boat was used to transport tools, equipment and supplies like building and sharp sand, plus cement, can be just seen over the stop gate.

Park head Deep Lock, Netherton. Again we see waterway wall restoration during a stoppage in 1934. At least ten men are busy knocking away defective brickwork, while another group look like they are taking a break on the balance beam, a perfect seat. And of course there are always the onlookers.

I went through this lock recently, on the B.C.N. society's boat Phoenix, *and the view is very much the same, though the distant viaduct is obscured somewhat by a line of trees. The Pumping House on the right became a steel stockholders for a time, but at the present, it is being utilised by the Dudley Canal Trust, and has their sign affixed to the facing wall. The lock house in the distance to the left is also extant. Notice the heavy concrete coping stones ready for laying, and also the thickness of the brickwork.*

Thomas's boat was the *Nansen 11*. It had a centre cockpit and was powered by a 30hp Ruston Hornsby. This was a three-cylinder nuisance, especially in cold weather when it was extremely difficult to start. The problem lay with the battery, which was sluggish in the cold and hadn't the strength to turn over the engine. The only alternative to get it going was by manpower. 'It took six of us, swinging two handles, to get this beast going on some days.' On occasions three boats worked together, one man per boat, bringing coal in to Birmingham from Walsall. 'After being on the boats for some years, my father also wanted a change, and strangely enough he went off with the bricklayers as a mate.'

George was also a restless young man, yearning for a change of scene. For a few years he left the canals for a variety of different jobs until the death of his father in 1949. George was still living at B.C.N. house 34 in Gas Street, but his mother, as a consequence of losing her husband, became anxious that she would also have to leave her home, which belonged to the company. George went to the depot at Icknield Port to discuss the situation with Mr Holt, who was now in charge. Mr Holt made it quite clear to George that he wanted him back, so George packed in his present job, and returned to the depot. The men's pay at this time was around thirty-five shillings and fourpence per week. The rent on the house was four shillings and sixpence per week.

Icknield Port Maintenance Depot. There was a boat shed, carpenters' workshop, stores, paintshop (and glazing), blacksmiths, house and garage. Thomas Price was gaffer in the early 1940s, followed by Dick Holt. The wooden wheel barrow with the straight back legs was strengthened by a metal ferule that was heated and then shrunk onto the wood. Jack Aston, the foreman carpenter, is behind the barrow. George's push-bike, has the white mudguard. Heavy horse boxes in the foreground were used as supports for carpenters work. The garage is on the right, the stores behind Jack. These buildings are still there, but their future is undecided.

The depot had a lorry and George, fancying his chances, asked if he could learn to drive it. British Waterways, in Sherbourn Street at that time, were starting to use a small fleet of lorries, and George transported goods from the Stourport basin.

Now retired, George lives in a flat in Sherborne Wharf with his wife Jean, and on occasions he takes school parties around the canal loops close to the city centre, thereby communicating his own special knowledge and experiences.

Birmingham Brindley Place, 1999. Part of the re-developed city centre. The canal plays the perfect focal point for shopping and leisure.

Windmill End & Bumble Hole, Netherton.

Contours from the Rowley ridge, drop steeply down to the Rowley road, and then continue on a tumbling course over an undulating landscape into Darby and Windmill End. The view from the present car park at Warrens Hall Park formerly Warrens Hall Colliery (see map) is vast and embracing. From Darby End, with Netherton church on our right, the land continues its gentle fall toward Merry Hill, Stourbridge and Kidderminster. To the distant left are the Clent Hills, while far away on the skyline is Woodbury and Abberley Hills, just the other side of Stourport. To the right are the Clee hills.

The scene immediately below us is that of a recovered landscape. Nature has clothed the once intense industrial workings of less than 100 years ago with grass, trees and shrubs. Only the ruins of Cobbs engine house, and the canal itself, show evidence of a world gone by. The accompanying map of 1884, depicts an altogether different scene. Covering an area of less than one square mile, we find thirteen separate collieries with their shafts and tunnels, while another five are no more than 300 yards away. Note that each of these are operating more than one

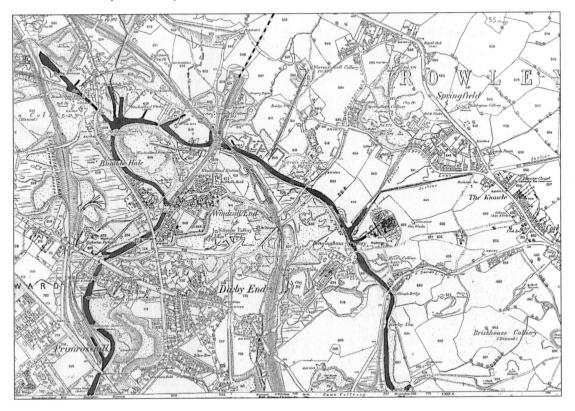

working shaft, Saltwells Colliery for instance has at least twenty-nine shafts, though not necessarily all in this area. The positions of the shafts do not begin to help us see the extent of the underground workings, which must be extensive. In fact any self-respecting colony of rabbits, would surely congratulate themselves on such a maze of tunnels. It is most apt that one them is named 'Warrens Hall'.

Add to this scene, the claypits, two brickworks, furnaces and iron works, and we start to conjure up an image that Thomas Tancred wrote about in 1843, when he described the Black Country as 'An endless village, intermingled with blazing furnaces, heaps of burning coal, piles of iron stone calcining, forges, pit banks, engine chimneys, countless foundries and factories, an area criss crossed with canals.'

Cobbs Engine house. Or to give it its correct title Windmill End Pumping Station.

Our canal here, is the Dudley No.2 that opened in 1798. The convoluted section (in black) is roughly in the middle of an eleven mile canal, that linked the No.1 at Park Head, with the Birmingham-Worcester canal at Selly Oak, via the Lapal tunnel. It enters the map at Primrose Hill, after hugging the 453ft contour around Netherton hill. The prominent church at the top of the hill is St Andrews, where the graveyard contains victims from the cholera outbreak that hit the Black Country in the mid-1800s. There are two and a half miles of canal on this map including arms and basins, and the entrance to the Netherton tunnel. In 1858, when the tunnel was constructed, a new section was taken across the Bumble Hole loop, thus cutting it off, and today only the southern portion is still in water. The junctions are gracefully crossed by cast iron bridges from the Toll End Works. They are from the same date as the tunnel, as is the matching pair at the other end.

Cobbs Engine House

The substantial remains of this classic pumping house, where once lived and breathed a mighty steam engine, now stands as a central picturesque feature of Warrens Hall park. The main building and chimney, can easily be reached from the car park, off the Rowley Road, Dudley (not far from the Cross Keys pub, or from the Windmill End Visitors Centre at Netherton). This simple, three storey, red brick building is now protected as a scheduled ancient monument, thanks to the hard work of people like George Price, and stands as a silent but potent testimony to the sounds and activities of the not too distant past. The thickness of its walls alone, point to its workmanlike past.

The purpose of the engine and building, erected in about 1830, was to pump as much water out of the nearby mines as possible. The accompanying picture shows how it used to be before the engines were taken away, and the shafts were filled in for safety reasons.

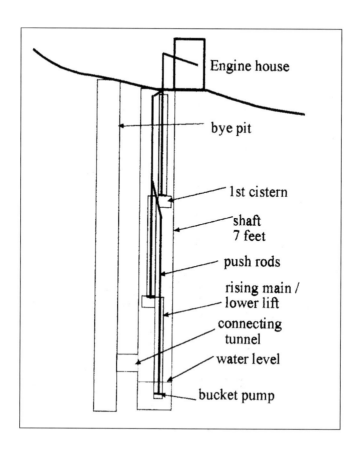

Engine house

bye pit

1st cistern

shaft
7 feet

push rods

rising main /
lower lift

connecting
tunnel

water level

bucket pump

1. The Bye Pit headframe (a bye pit was a secondary shaft near the main one).
2. Pumping shaft headframe.
3. Engine house.
4. Boiler house.
5. Chimney stack.
6. Winding engine house (only the engine house and stack are extant).

Very close to the main pumping house, were two parallel shafts or wells, from which water was extracted. The final depth was about 520ft, and terminated in a sump area where water was allowed to collect. This depth had been increased several times over the years, reflecting the depth to which coal was being worked toward the end of the engine's life. In the vicinity of Windmill End there was a variety of coal quality to be found, all at differing depths. At 189ft was the best, or brooch coal, at 387ft the thick coal (this was the renowned 30ft seam that delineated the 'Black Country'). Heathen coal was at 412ft, while the new mine coal (the latest to be dug) was found at 477ft.

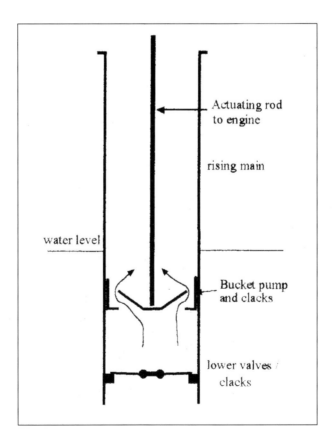

How was the water raised?

Water was drawn from the sump in three stages, by a large bore, cast iron pipe system, known as a rising main. At the bottom of each rising main was a bucket lift that operated with a set of valves called clacks. The first diagram (not to scale) shows the overall arrangement. The rising mains pipes were flanged and bolted 14ft lengths, having an internal diameter of 15in.

This diagram shows the working barrel, that had a half inch brass lining, and bucket pump at the bottom of each section of rising main. A seal was made between that and the bucket pump with oiled leather, and spare buckets were always on hand to be quickly changed, though it must have been a perilous task, to have gone all the way down there via a ladder system, and accessed the worn one by way of a bolted hatch. With each lift, the buckets' clacks would close, the lower clacks open, and water would be drawn between. As the bucket descended, its clacks would open, the lower ones would be shut, and water would be forced on top of the bucket. The bucket would then continue to lift a column of water to the intermediate cistern, and up to the surface. Our pumping engine was now ready to fulfil two important functions. Not only was it emptying the mines, but the water pumped out, helped to top up the local canals.

The bucket pump was able to lift out 43gal. for every stroke, at eight strokes per minute this resulted in a possible 495,000gal. a day. Figures for the period of 1917-1920 show that approximately 367,000gal. per day were going into the canal, and the B.C.N. were paying 6d per lock full (around 30,000gal.). When you take into consideration that the canal from here on, was continually emptying itself down the Dudley Nos 1 & 2, Stourbridge and Staffs & Worcester canals, and finally into the Severn, it must be said that the mines at Windmill End, were a useful source of water.

On the earlier pencil drawing, you will see at the left a horse gin, which was a primitive form of winding gear. A large drum, fitted with a cable was set horizontally, so that a horse (or horses) could walk around in circles, lowering or raising the pit gear.

The Pumping Engine

This early engine, of the James Watt, single acting/condensing type, was an atmospheric engine, where steam was fed into a large piston and cylinder arrangement, and cooled to create a partial vacuum. Atmospheric pressure at the top of the piston would force it down, thus rocking the enormous beam that was suspended toward the top of the engine house. The engine, though receiving modifications throughout its life of nearly 100 years, was therefore very different in design to the high pressure steam engines of later years, when steam was injected via valves, either side of an enclosed piston (double acting).

Our earlier drawing actually shows two engine houses, only one of which survives. The smaller building in front of the stack, housed a second atmospheric engine that was used to lower men and equipment down the shaft. It was this engine that was eventually packed and sent to the Ford Museum at Dearborn, Michigan. The larger pumping engine eventually went as scrap. But, thanks to the efforts of folk like George Price, the stack and main building have been saved for future generations.

Details:

Fuel used on the boilers was coal slack, and the boilers consumed about fifty tons per week, though the cost for this was minimal because of its relationship with the mine only yards away. The mine was known as the Windmill End No.3 and Warrens Hall collieries.

Engine stroke 10ft at the engine, 7ft at the working shaft Beam 20ft long.

A recent photograph shows the stack and main engine house as it appears today (1999)

Windmill End and its Boatmen

The visitor centre at Windmill End, Netherton, has become a regular meeting spot for three old boatmen at least. Gathering there, especially on a pleasant summer day when they can sit outside have tea and watch the world go by, are Jack, Joe and William. Jack Edgington is the oldest, being born in 1919, and he has had a notable life, not just on the canals but also in the 8th Army during the Second World War, when he served in the desert campaign against Rommel. The war separated into two halves a rather long working life on the Black Country canals that effectively commenced when he was seventeen.

In 1937, two years before war broke out, Jack started with the family business of Ben Rounds in Windmill End, where his father, John, worked as a boatman. Rounds was one of many boating firms that the canal system had gainfully employed over the years. All three of Ben's sons worked alongside their father in the business. Jack started work with one of those sons. Part of the week they transported goods on lorries, the rest of it was spent on a boat.

The lorry used at this time was a Fordson, the loads were winched on and off with a hand-winding gear. Boat trips were mostly from Wallace Wharf near Holly Hall, where coal from Baggeridge mines was shipped to Doulton's, the ceramics firm, near Windmill End. Wallace wharf was at the end of the Pensnett Canal (now lost), a short arm, less than two miles long, that ran off the Dudley No.1 canal, from a junction above Park Head locks. The Pensnett Canal was a private arm, owned by the Earl of Dudley, and the wharf was at the end of this watery cul-de sac, next to Hartshill bus garage. 'When the coal was loaded' Jack said. 'You had to get it right. It was no good just putting it all in one spot'.

The coal had to be loaded evenly into four piles along the length of the boat, particularly when using wooden boats. These piles were known as rucks, and the practice prevented the possible break up of the boat. The user of much of this coal (it was in fact slack, a fine powdery form of coal) was Doulton's, at that time a huge company, producing ceramic ware for kitchens and bathrooms.

Jack immediately joined up when the war started, and saw it through to its finish, but not without injury. During one artillery assault in North Africa, he and a handful of soldiers were in a house that was shelled by the Germans. The house came crashing down around them, and Jack was wounded on his back and arm. His Sergeant lost a leg in that particular attack. After a few weeks care in the hospital in Rimini, Jack was well enough to return to his regiment.

When the hostilities ended in 1945, Jack returned to Netherton, and Rounds, which was continuing as before. The pace of life however, and the pace of transport, had increased dramatically over the five hectic war years, and this had a knock on effect on the way goods were transported from one place to another.

It was as though the two world wars had speeded up the way society operated, and it was obvious that the canals were unable to move goods fast enough. As late as 1947 it seemed that there was plenty of carrying work, but itwould, in the next decade or so, move from narrow boats to lorry, never to come back.

Firms small and large still operated horse powered boats, ('Osses' as they were called in the Black Country) and Jack, Joe and William have memories, fond and otherwise, of these marvellous animals. Generally speaking the 'Osses' were good tempered, and were essential members of the team, almost friends. But horses have personalities, and there were some real sods, the men being very careful how they treated those particularly temperamental creatures. Jack himself fell foul of one named Maggie, a black mare. It was Maggie, who being in a bit of a bad mood day that day, decided out of complete malice, to kick Jack in the groin. This extremely unpleasant injury put him in bed for a fortnight.

When men moved from one boat to another, the practice in this and other firms was to take your tiller, helm, mast and personal effects with you. Coal or slack was the usual commodity being moved at this time, and many trips were made to the colliery at Hednesford (near Cannock), and then back past Wolverhampton, along the New Main line, and on to Gibbons and Bodnam at Rotton Park Street, almost in Birmingham. Less notable trips simply brought rubbish back to Windmill End, from where it was taken away by lorry.

After two or three years with Rounds, Jack made his last move to Stewart & Lloyds, in nearby Halesowen. When I asked why he made the move, Jack simply replied 'The money was better'. Stewarts & Lloyds were a big firm that manufactured tubing and they kept a large fleet of 'Maybe an 'undred' narrow boats', Jack recalls, 'No names, just numbers'. After an interview with Mr Franklin, where Jack related his boating experience, he started on the coal runs.

For a short time he used an iron day boat with a small cabin, still hauled by horse. Shortly after, Stewarts & Lloyds introduced diesel tugs, and Jack moved on to one of those, No.2. Trips were now over to Hamstead Colliery, entailing a run into Birmingham, down the Farmers Bridge 'Thirteen' to Salford Junction, and then along the Tame Valley canal. Other runs were over to Cannock Chase, and the usual start time, was 3:30 a.m. If everything went well, i.e. loading, and the using of any locks, then they may have arrived back in Windmill End by seven thirty in the evening. A long day indeed!

No.2 tug was a forty footer, equipped with a twin cylinder National diesel engine, and it pulled two and sometimes three butties. Jack remembers that these engines were generally pretty good, though they could be a little difficult to start in cold weather. To get it going, a starting handle was put in place and the engine had to be cranked as fast as possible. Then the decompression switch was dropped, and if you got it right, away it would go.

Occasionally it appeared that some of the idiosyncrasies of its equine predecessors had been passed on, and the engine would kick back with malice, resulting in a rather painful wrist, and Jack has even known a handle to break.

Dennis Fellows is a little younger than our three Windmill End Veterans. However he still hails from the same neck of the woods, and has his own tale to tell of the Tunnel at Netherton. Dennis is definitely a Black Country character, when I met him in 1998 he had found himself the perfect job, as blacksmith at the Black Country Museum. He can still be found, with his wife, pottering around the Black Country canals on their respective narrow boats.

His recollections and love of the canals go back to the days just after the end of the last war when he was a lad attending school in Netherton (some of the time). Dennis admitted to me that he had no love for school and maths was the most hated subject of all. No doubt it was this dreaded loathing of school that made him skive off and head for the excitement and pleasure of the local canal and its boating activities. His first boat ride was on a horse drawn craft out of the depot at Brierley Hill. For several weeks he had been simply soaking up the atmosphere, walking along the towpath, following the boats, and getting to know the local crews, and now that investment was about to be rewarded.

How marvellous this ride was going to be, surging along through those dark mysterious waters at a steady four miles an hour, open sky, not a classroom in sight, and a powerful animal in front at the end of the towrope. The boat that day was *Saturn*, part of an ex-Shropshire Union fleet, then owned by the LMS (London, Midland & Scottish Railway). This particular boat was kept at their Brierley Hill depot, at the bottom of Mill Street. The LMS had two depots in the area, the other being the Primrose depot in Netherton. *Saturn*'s sister craft were also named after planets.

Our three Boatmen (and possibly a female admirer?) taking it easy outside the visitor centre at Bumble Hole. From left to right; Jack Edgington, Joe Chilton and William Jones.

91

Excitement ran high, as a young Dennis remembers, and he clambered on board for the first time and headed North, away from the Delph locks, toward Bumble Hole and the ominous Southern portal of the Netherton tunnel.

Breakfast for the two boatmen and their small companion that morning was fried tomatoes and horse meat steak, which was a popular meat of the day. Dennis says it tastes just like beef steak, but has a slight silver sheen to the uncooked flesh. After being inside the tunnel for well over half an hour, which to a young boy must have seemed much longer, they emerged into the Netherton Branch, the short stretch of water that leads up to Telford's New Main Line. Turning right at this junction, they journeyed for about a mile toward Birmingham before turning sharp left at the Pudding Green junction.

The final destination on this short haul trip was the Albion interchange basin in Great Bridge. The boat was unloaded, to be followed by a return journey, back through the tunnel, to a well deserved 'lamping' from his mother for missing school. Between 1948-1954, Dennis managed to get out onto the cut at least two or three times a month. He learned that the boatmen were named Sammy Waugh and Kia Smith and they taught their little helper how to operate the lock paddles. By doing this and other little jobs he earned himself a bag of coal (or two) which was transported home on the front of a butcher's bicycle.

As time went by it became possible to identify each boat by the different designs at the front and back, and the boatmen started to take Dennis further afield. During school holidays they went as far as the East Cannock basin to collect coal. This entailed a trip through the tunnel again, but this time turning left onto the main line and heading for Wolverhampton. The boat would proceed to Horseley Fields Junction, turn right onto the Curly Wurly (the Wyrley and Essington canal) and then left at Pelsall Junction onto the Cannock Extension Canal. Sometimes on a Friday Dennis would help take all the empty boats backwards down the Delph flight of locks and into the brickyard.

Work was physically demanding for men and women, who did most of the handballing of the heavy furnace bricks in and out of the boats, which they used to throw to each other three at a time. Coal was often loaded into the boats from overhead hoppers but it had to be shovelled out at the other end.

Dennis recalls vividly the day Sam and Kia received a new horse from the Netherton depot. The horse's behaviour was fine until he entered the tunnel, at which point he became increasingly difficult to handle. By the time they were at the first air shaft, the horse was in an emotional state, it jumped over the iron hand rail and dropped into the inky black waters of the canal. Kia quickly cut the towrope and Sammy led the horse along the bed of the canal until they got to the other end. It certainly wasn't a good start to the day, and they were well behind schedule. They persevered however, and managed to get the animal out of the water, placing a crude plaster on its underside where it had caught the rail in its frantic desire to escape. The bricks were eventually delivered to Bloomfield in Tipton, and then it was back to the Delph. This time, after passing the gauging stop just underneath the Tividale aqueduct, Sam decided to

Joe Chilton in 1949, taking the materials boat to a stoppage. The Lodge farm horse was 'Tom'. Notice the horse's gear, including collar, aimes, spreader, spoles and driving rein.

put a cloth sack over the horse's head, equipped with a couple of holes for its ears. This worked extremely well, and the bag was removed at the last air hole, resulting in a successful return journey, and a much happier horse.

Joe Chilton also worked for the firm of Ben Rounds after the Second World War, probably due to the fact that he had married one of Ben's daughters back in 1943. Most of Rounds' work concentrated on canal haulage, but they were sensible enough to run several trucks, and Joe recalls seeing such lost names as Dodge and Bean. (Bean's was a local Tipton Company and one of their cars is in the Black Country Museum). The unusual feature of these vehicles however, was their ability to change their outward appearance and function, and the men regularly took away the lorry upper structure, replacing it with a coach body. This was then used for passenger transport. A point to show that boats have a place in peoples hearts that lorries can never take, is suitably illustrated by the fact that the boats had names, the trucks never did. Rounds' day boats, were all named after family members, and there was *John, Bill, Joan, Margaret* and *Grace* to name a few (can you imagine a lorry named 'John'?).

Many of the boat runs were local, such as loading coke at Park Head, taking it down what the men called 'the sixteen', the Stourbridge Locks, and delivering to a factory not far from the bottom lock. In 1948, Joe went to work for British Waterways, and he lived at No.7 Canal Side Cottages. These buildings can be seen on the early maps of the area displayed at the Bumble Hole Visitor Centre. Next door to Joe lived Jake Elwell, who happened to be the tunnel keeper (the southern portal of the Netherton tunnel is only a few hundred yards up the towpath). Jake's job, and in fact his reason to be, was to inspect the tunnel each day. At 6 a.m. he could be seen entering the mouth of the tunnel, usually equipped with a wheel barrow and a set of tools, and he would walk the tunnel to the other end at Tividale, returning by the opposite towpath (the Netherton tunnel at 3,027yards, is roughly one and three quarter miles long and this walk would take Jake at least an hour in one direction). On the way he would inspect the walls, towpath, lighting (which was electric at this time) and the hand rail. Under normal conditions a hand rail would last some time, but we have to remember that much of the traffic was pulled by horses, and when a towrope is wet it picks up grit and becomes extremely

Routine summer maintenance on the canal banks, 1950. Joe and Tommy Hughes are not far from Blackbrook bridge, Netherton. The job in hand is face puddling, where the men have to first clear away weeds, and then get down to the impervious clay lining. All along the towpath, behind the men, and on the barrow, are piles of new clay, ready to be to be softened and trod into place. Joe has in his hand a clay bat, used to batter down and smooth off the clay.

Winter 1951, and a disaster in the making. Construction of the blocks of flats on the right has undermined the canal bank, and the breach behind the waterway wall can clearly be seen.

Same breach but looking the other way, toward Lodge Farm bridge.

abrasive. So, coupled with the continual wearing of passing taut towropes, and the perpetually damp conditions in the tunnel causing oxidation, removal and replacement of sections of the hand rail was an ongoing job.

By 1953 the condition of the tunnel's lights and the electrical cables was extremely poor and there were constant faults. The decision was taken to remove the whole system. Joe, along with others, worked to take it out. Operating from a boat with a working platform, Joe's gang went from one end to the other and removed the lot. At this point in the discussion, Jack butted in with 'There were seventy-two lights in that tunnel you know'. Falling into the trap I asked 'And how do you know that Jack?' 'Cus I counted em, that's how.' was the reply. I suppose that little comment illustrates the point well, there is very little else to do in a dark tube for over half an hour, except count the lights.

During the late 1940s, Joe was working as a lengthsman or ganger from the Lodge Farm depot. Tasks included hedge laying, box and face puddling and towpath repairs. Some of the other workers at that time included Tommy Hughs, Edwin Walker and Geoff Downing. Usually there was a small gang of them working on projects together but, on big jobs like stoppages, many other hands from around the Black Country would be drafted in to help out. Joe and his mates could then easily be joined by another fifty or sixty blokes. One year, they built an overflow weir. This was designed to take excess water off the Dudley No.1 Canal and into the brook only a few yards away. The name of this tiny tributary was Mouseweet Brook, don't you just love it? I think it goes marvellously well with its neighbours Bumble Hole and Windmill End.

William Jones, the third member of our Bumble Hole group, is also getting along in years, being born in 1927. William, like many boatmen of that era, followed another member of the family on to the cut. In this case it was his stepfather Thomas Alliband. Thomas worked for the LMS from their Primrose depot, situated at the top of the Cradley road, just outside Netherton. The Primrose Depot was an extremely active narrowboating base, where there were stables for twenty-six horses, and a warehouse. William told me that you could find all manner of goods in and around the warehouse, including items such as corn, finished clothing, cloth in bales, pots and pans and even Guinness in wooden barrels. All of this stuff was waiting to be transhipped from rail to boat or vice versa. During the war years, the majority of boat trips from the

Repairs to the puddle. The only worker we were able to recognise, was the man on the left, who is Alf Mole. Birchills toll house, Walsall, is in the background.

Primrose Depot were short haul, often less than ten miles and some as little as three or four, and William made many of those to the Albion interchange basin in Great Bridge or over to Bloomfield in Tipton.

Starting at five in the morning, William would arrive at the depot and collect a boat that had been loaded during the night. That loading was always done by a team of women, and the only aid that these Black Country Amazons had was a couple of hand winches, a case of 'winches and wenches' you might say. After the war, the LMS continued to use horses for boat haulage and they tended to be of the short stocky variety, around 15/2 to 15/3 hands. The local dredger was however pulled by what the men called a 'Moke' or mule. Horses were generally reliable, even friendly and sociable beasts (though there was always the exception). William, Jack and Joe remember (with a smile) that the mules were, on many occasions, difficult critters to handle. Then he related to me a mule tale, perfectly illustrating the contrary nature of those animals.

Three other canal workers, Jack Duffield, Tim Hipkiss and Ernie Heritage, used a mule to pull their cart (the mule belonged to Ernie). One day they were returning to Netherton from Dudley and had to negotiate the island at the top of Trindle Road. The mule enjoyed going around the island so much that it persisted in going around it several times, before they could persuade it to head off for Netherton. On other occasions the mules would find the dirtiest puddle they could, and lie down and roll in it, stopping only when *they* had had enough.

In 1944 William went to work for Noah Hingley's. This was one of the biggest iron founders and chain makers in the area. Hingley's had their own boats, plus two tugs, and they were advantageously placed for canal haulage, having their own wharf on the Dudley No.2 canal, next to the Halesowen road, Netherton (less than half a mile along the canal from Windmill End).

Sneyd Junction. B.C.N. houses on left. Ice breaker in foreground, with two masts.

Spoon dredger, with from left to right; Charlie James, possibly Ruben Darby's son, Ruben Darby and Tom Feakey. Notice the semi-circular 'spoon' being tipped of its contents into the boat.

Noah Hingley's is well known in the Black Country for making the anchor and chain for what is probably the most famous ship of all time, the White Star liner RMS *Titanic*. On Saturday 6 May 1911 the headline of the local newspaper read 'The Biggest Anchor In The World'. And indeed it was, with a length of 18ft 6in, and a width of 10ft 9in, it weighed almost sixteen tons. Hingley's, like many Black Country concerns at this time, used prodigious amounts of coal and this was all brought in by boat from a variety of pits.

William's week, started at around 3 a.m. on Monday morning, his first destination was the Walsall Wood Colliery near Brownhills. They had the use of a tug, equipped with a Lister engine, and this would pull three, or sometimes four, day boats, each boat with its own steerer. On arriving at Pelsall Junction, one of the boats would continue on to a second colliery. This meant that its steerer would have to bow haul it for half a mile, then after loading he would punt it from the rear with a shaft, until he met up with the tug again.

At the colliery, the boats were loaded from tubs, each containing 30cwt, until they were laden to 26tons. This particular journey was made using the Wolverhampton canal as far as Horseley Fields Junction, and then the Wyrley and Essington canal up to Pelsall Junction. In Netherton, they unloaded at Bonepit wharf, some distance from Hingley's, because Hingley's wharf wasn't long enough to deal with the vast quantities of coal arriving each day.

As a consequence, many of the boats off loaded at Bonepit wharf, close to St Peters church, and then the coal travelled the final leg on Bedford lorries. The men were paid four pounds per trip. On Wednesdays, they often went over to the Holly Bank Colliery near Essington (Wolverhampton). Other local pits used by Hingley's included the Sandwell Park Colliery. Their loading chutes were located on the Old main line near Smethwick. This pit, and its neighbour, the Jubilee colliery, was some distance away from the canal, with coal being brought to the wharf on a rail line. The concrete loading chutes can still be seen today as can the little hut on the towpath where the boatmen used to shelter, and William remembers sitting in there when it was raining. After loading it was back to Windmill End. On Friday they would return to the pit at Essington. This was more or less the boating routine while working for Hingley's just after the war.

As the years passed, William got a bit fed up with boating (his own words) and in 1952 he went trucking, travelling all over the country. Nevertheless the lure of the canals stayed with him and, after two years away, he returned to Hingley's on the regular coal runs, with the same routine as before. As he was chatting to Jack one day, William learned that the money was considerably better at Stewarts & Lloyds, so after a short interview with Len Green, the foreman, he started there. It is interesting to note that as late as the 1950s, Stewarts & Lloyds still operated over 100 narrow boats.

The trade was of course the same; coal, coal and more coal, and there were still the early starts at around 3.30 a.m., but at least the destinations were different. Stewarts & Lloyds tended to have their coal from the Cannock Chase collieries, but sometimes it was coke from Windsor Street in Birmingham, or maybe Swan Village (between West Bromwich and Great Bridge). Tugs did the hauling, pulling a train of two to four boats. Even though the majority of trips were short haul, there were occasions when the men had to spend a night in the Spartan conditions of the cabin. Jack interrupted at this point with. 'You had three coats. One for wearin', one for sleepin' on, and another for when it was rainin'.' No soft beds in those days, just hard wooden boards to drop your weary body onto at the end of a long day.

And on that final note of 'Boy was it tough when I was a lad' (and I am sure that it was), I left our three fine old gents to finish their tea and biscuits.

The Dudley and Netherton Tunnels

The Black Country neighbours of Tipton, Wednesbury and West Bromwich, are geographically separated from their industrial cousins, Brierley Hill and Cradley Heath, by a long ridge of high ground. Starting just outside Wolverhampton, this ridge runs diagonally, north west to south east, through Sedgley, Dudley and Rowley Regis, before dropping down to Blackheath. Staying around 200metres (just over 600ft) it rises to 271metres (876ft) at Turners Hill (Rowley) where there are excellent views of the old Black Country. This high ground, dominated the land around it by some 450ft, and was a formidable obstacle to any canal system. Were the early canal engineers and developers going to be stopped by this? Absolutely not. The use of locks was out of the question, the sides were too steep, too long, and there was no room for a summit pound, that is, if water could have been persuaded to get up there. Still, this $1\frac{1}{2}$mile wide hill was to be pierced not once, but twice in the space of 100 years, so that narrow boats could save a day's journey by going around its bulk. This is a tribute to the determination of the tunnel's supporters and promoters, and the courage and strength of its excavators, of whom we know little.

The map shows that the Dudley and Netherton tunnels are only $1\frac{1}{2}$ miles apart, that they are amazingly parallel, and they are of a similar length, though there is some controversy over which is the longer. This is due to the fact that the Dudley is really a series of tunnels. But the similarity ends there, because their internal dimensions, and the time and manner in which they were built, differ greatly. The first tunnel to be cut was of course the Dudley, though it must be added that the final tunnel going from Tipton through to Park Head, was proceeded by a much shorter tunnel that bored into the hillside under Dudley and its castle. These were the limestone workings owned by Lord Dudley.

Following the completion of the Wolverhampton to Birmingham canal in 1772, one of the biggest landowners and industrialists in the Black Country was the 2nd Lord Viscount of Dudley. He saw the potential of connecting his prosperous limestone production, which had a market in agriculture and industry, to this new, efficient means of transportation less than half a mile away at Tipton Green. A short branch was cut that came to be known as Lord Ward's Canal. This included a 226yd tunnel that terminated under Castle hill. $1\frac{1}{2}$ miles away, on the southern side of the Dudley ridge, where Lord Ward and others were actively engaged in coal extraction. In 1779, this area of Dudley became connected to the Staffordshire and Worcestershire canal

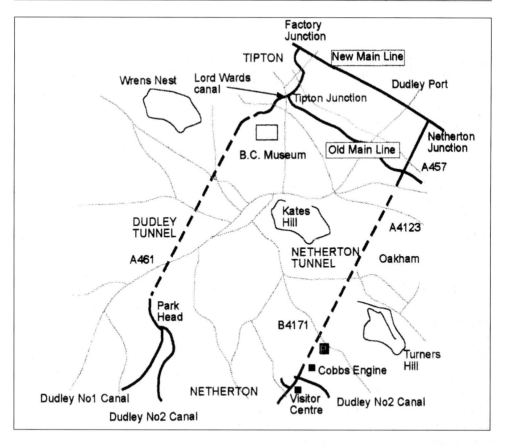

(1772) via the Dudley No.1 canal and the Stourbridge, at Stourton Junction. Thus there were now two busy canal systems either side of the ridge, and it made sense to join them, especially as a 226yd start had already been made. Five years went by, and in 1784 steps were taken to complete the tunnel. A survey was conducted by John Snape, assisted by Samuel Bull. The estimated cost was £18,000. The dimensions of the bore were to be a height of 14ft, and a width of 9ft. When the five feet of water was introduced however, the height above water would be only 9ft, very often much less, making conditions dark, extremely claustrophobic and allowing only one way working. Like other early tunnels there was no plan for a towpath and boats were to be legged through. This was a process where the men lay on their backs on the boat (usually on a board across the width of the boat), placed their feet on the wall or roof of the tunnel and literally walked the boat from one of the tunnel to the other.

The tunnel's line was laid out over the top of the hill, using simple techniques that had been utilised on other tunnels. Long poles were knocked into the ground at regular distances, and aligned by eye (this is really quite accurate). From this line shafts were sunk to the required depth, some lined with brick as they went down, much like a well. At the bottom of each shaft the excavation of the tunnel was started in both directions called headings.

The Dudley tunnel had about twelve shafts, while the later Netherton had seventeen. This meant that men were digging (and sometimes blasting) their way along from twenty-six or thirty-six points respectively (not forgetting the entrance cuttings). To ensure that the headings were going in the right direction, the line strung across the top of the shaft was transferred to the base, by dropping two plumb lines, as far apart as the width of the shaft would allow.

After allowing the weights to settle, the men at the bottom of the shaft would hopefully be working to the same line as the men above. Mistakes in measurements and directions were sometimes made, resulting in a not so perfect line. The most serious that I have come across, is in the tunnel at Braunston on the Grand Union canal, where incompetence by the engineer has left a permanent kink in the middle. He had his pay halved for this error.

As the tunnel was dug, spoil from down below was hauled up the shafts by horse-powered gins. When the tunnel was completed some of these shafts were left for ventilation purposes, while others were filled in. The construction of the Dudley tunnel was, like others, not without its problems. These included incompetent contractors (John Pinkerton was the worst), the loss of the original chief engineer, difficult terrain, and water in the workings. Well over budget, and long overdue, the Dudley was finally opened in June 1792, but boats had to wait another four months until the Birmingham Gazette made the formal announcement on 15 October. So from start to finish, the Dudley took seven long years of backbreaking labour. The Netherton, on the other hand, having a similar length, but with a vastly increased bore and twin

Exiting Netherton Tunnel, South Portal.

towpaths, took only two and a half years, thus demonstrating the advances that had been made in tunnel excavation during the early rail years. The question is, why was a second tunnel required? Size is the simple answer. The Dudley tunnel just wasn't built big enough to take an increase in traffic.

So if the Dudley had been built to the dimensions of the Netherton, where there is room for boats to pass each other, the growing numbers of users could have been accommodated. But by the 1830s a new tunnel was desperately needed to cope with the great increase in boating traffic.

The Netherton Tunnel

By 1832 the Birmingham Canal Navigation Company possessed 157 miles of canal. Of this 52.5miles were on the Wolverhampton level (473ft), 34.5miles on the Birmingham level (453ft), and twenty miles on the Walsall level. Even though the fledgling railways were taking a cut of the carrying trade, 1,492,000 tons of coal alone, were being moved by narrow boats. By 1854 it was 3.1million tons, a doubling in just over twenty years. The Dudley tunnel was 3,200yards long, between 8 and 9ft wide, with around 6 to 9feet above water level. Leggers were paid 3s 6d (17.5 new pence) per trip, which took about $3\frac{1}{2}$hours. On occasions there were as many as 100 boats waiting to go through.

Records for boats passing through the Dudley are: 1845, 25,916 boats; 1853, 41,704 boats; 1854, 39,025 boats, carrying 438,000 tons. The drop in the number of boats using the tunnel in 1854 was due to a dry season, and the depth of water in the tunnel could not be maintained. Boats using the tunnel sometimes had to unload a part of the cargo, and this was most unsatisfactory.

Complaints came in from the coal and iron masters. Proposals for a new tunnel, an Act and Royal Assent, followed. Drawings for the Netherton were undertaken by Messrs Walker, Burgess and Cooper. In November the contract for the works was given to Mr George Meakin of Birkenhead. Mr Walker was to be the resident engineer, with seven inspectors of works under him, the chief of whom was James Sager. A practical start was made when the first sod was removed by Lord Ward at shaft No.7 on 28 December 1855, and on 17 January the following year the first shaft was under way. The tunnel itself was commenced on 15 March at shaft No.15, and on 4 April the first brick was laid. Mr Walker himself laid the final brick, in the archway between shafts 7 and 8 on 25 March 1858. The tunnel was open to traffic on 20 August, a remarkable total of only thirty-two months. During this very busy time, the tunnel, with its two brick portals and its two canal approaches plus the embankments, were finished.

In total there were $2\frac{1}{2}$miles of canal (the tunnel was approximately $1\frac{3}{4}$miles of that) along with its puddle, waterway wall and towpaths and there are twin towpaths on each approaching canal section to complement the tunnels.

The approach to the Southern end of the tunnel, via Windmill End. Toll End bridges adorn the junctions, while Cobb's engine house sits silently on the hillside. The visitor centre is on the right.

Tunnel Specifics

The total amount of puddling clay used to render the tunnel and canal waterproof was 53,000 cubic yards, and on the puddle at the bottom, a layer of furnace cinders 6in thick was laid to protect the puddle from damage. To protect the WaterWay Walls inside the tunnel, cast iron plates were affixed, that were 12ft long, 9in wide and $^{3}/_{4}$in thick. They weighed a massive 288lbs each, not something you would like dropped on your toe. These plates dovetailed into each other and were keyed into the Waterway wall.

The walls of the towing path were also placed on puddle, and care was taken because of settlement. Brickwork was laid to a height of no more than 18in at a time. It was allowed to stand for several days before more courses were added.

Towpaths and Shafts

The towing paths received 6in of burnt red ashes from the local puddling furnaces, and this made a durable horse road (so said Mr Walker himself) and this expression struck a chord with me, because even in the 1950s and 1960s I remember people in the Black Country referring to the highways as horse roads. As mentioned earlier, seventeen shafts were dug for the construction of the Netherton, and the distances between them varied from 164 to 200yards. From this number, ten were to be used only in construction, and on completion of the tunnel they were filled in. Seven were to be left for ventilation. Four of the temporary shafts were timber lined, the rest were brick and they were 9ft by 8ft. The permanent shafts were all brick lined, and they had a diameter of 10ft, and the brickwork was 9in thick.

The diagram shows the approximate shapes, and thus areas, to scale, of the Netherton tunnel. Top; the Dudley (bottom left) and the headings made for the Netherton, which was essentially a corridor five feet by three feet. Then when the headings were all connected, the tunnel was widened out to the full bore, plus the area required for brickwork, to include towpaths and canal.

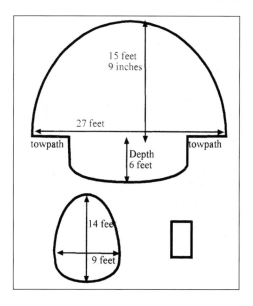

If you decide to go through the Netherton tunnel, and I recommend that you do, you will find that the remaining shafts are easily identified when you reach them, by a shower of water, and a minute dappling of light on the water's surface. If you glance up at the shafts, the brickwork can be seen supported by a cast iron curb weighing nine tons. For safety reasons after the tunnel's completion, the brickwork at the top of these remaining circular shafts was taken to a height of 12ft above ground, and topped with an iron grating. These can be seen today dotted at intervals over the hillside, and there is a fine example quite close to Bumble Hole if you want to have a look.

Deaths and Injuries

Tunnelling has always been a dangerous activity, and thankfully much has changed since the 1850s to protect people in the working environment. Following is a record of the more serious accidents that occurred during the construction of the Netherton.

Nine men were killed, and eighteen seriously injured, during those two and a half years. Or, in other words, there was a serious accident for every working month a poor record indeed. Of those killed, one man fell down shaft No.11, another was drowned in the sump of shaft No.7, five were killed by stones or other objects falling down the shafts onto them, and the other two by falling objects while they were in the process of mining.

Of those injured, two were pulled over the pulley at the top of shaft No.10, due to the complete carelessness of the engine operator. Twelve were hurt by falling stones etc. (eight down shafts, four mining). Two fell off scaffolding, and the other two were injured by machinery they were using on the surface.

It makes you wonder if many lives and accidents could have been saved by a little more care at the shaft mouth (maybe the fitting of toe boards) or the wearing of hard hats which everyone now has on construction sites. Don't forget that some of those shafts were between 100-200ft deep, and even a small stone falling that distance would do serious damage to an uncovered head.

Bricks and Mortar.

Earlier in the book we came across the Steward Aqueduct, which was in 1999 receiving repair to the brickwork. They used no cement in the mortar, as per original practice. Mr Walker's notes on the tunnel's brickwork, confirm that practice, even providing details of how the lime was prepared. The mortar mix was 4parts Hayhead lime (measured before being slacked), 4 sand and 1 ashes.

The lime was ground for twenty minutes under edge stones, during which time the sand, ashes and water were added. Four mortar pans, driven by a 20hp engine were erected at Tividale, and two, driven by a 12hp engine at Windmill End. This mortar was so good that it was used throughout, except on the occasions where work was required to set in a few hours.

The total quantity of bricks used on the tunnel and connecting canalwork, was 75,000cubic yards. The type of brick used, except in the faces of bridges and tunnel portals, were Staffordshire 'Browns'. Other brickwork was Staffordshire 'Blues'. Bricks were supplied from Old Hill, Tividale, Oldbury, Dudley Port, Netherton and Stourbridge. They were tested in pairs under pressures of between 14 and 31tons to ensure that they were of the very best quality.

Some bricks were moulded 'specials' for use in the invert and portals, the stone used was mainly a sandstone from Dukes quarry in Derbyshire. Due to the size of the undertaking, a wharf was constructed at either end of the tunnel and, for conveyance of materials to the shafts, a tramway with a gauge of 2ft 6in was laid over the top of the hillside, with passing places and sidings at each shaft. Carpenters, smiths, and fitting shops were erected at the Tividale end.

On a final note, it seems appropriate to remark on the accuracy with which the Netherton tunnel was built, especially when compared with other canal tunnels. I quote from the senior engineer Mr Walker, who wrote the report.

'The author is glad to be able to state, that no part of the tunnel was one inch out of the straight line; and when the water was admitted, the guards were found to be exactly level, this remark does not, however, now apply to a short piece of about three hundred feet, at the south end of the tunnel, where, as early as June 1857, it had been discovered and reported by the author, that a subsidence was going on from mining operations.'

This, of course, was rectified and we can still admire the skill, accuracy and hard work that went into the making of this remarkable tunnel almost 150 years ago, as we continue to use it on into the new millennium.

1952. One of the earliest pleasure trips through the Dudley tunnel. William King decided to organise an outing for family and friends. Well, things grew until three LMS boats were needed. A Matty tug was used for haulage. Will's young daughter Ruth was one of the crowd.

The Pumping Station at Bratch

The Pumping Station, Bratch, shortly after construction. The nearest room was for coal storage, the centre was the boiler house and the largest part contained the two pumping engines and water pumps. The original 90ft stack looks perfectly balanced, with its iron railings and weather cock, but sadly this feature has gone. Fortunately everything else is in good shape. Notice the tiny trees planted around the building, which are now huge.

Bratch, near Wombourn is known for two things; one is its set of locks, and the other is its Victorian pumping station. Both are unique in their own special way. The locks appear to be a staircase, though they are patently not, and the towers of the pumping station ought to appear in a book of fairy stories. These two little gems are only yards apart, but go together like peaches and cream. In fact with the Staffordshire and Worcestershire canal only yards away (a bit of good planning if ever I've seen it), coal could almost have been emptied straight into the boiler room. However, we're going to look specifically at the pumping station and answer some questions associated with it. Such as, who designed it, and why was it built? What sort of steam engines does it have, and what brought about their restoration?

There are many fine examples of Victorian industrial architecture throughout the Midlands, many associated with the canal system. To my mind, none outshine this wondrous example of the builder's and bricklayer's art from this period, than the water pumping station at Bratch. Every year, hundreds of tourists, many of those going north or south on the southern half of the loveliest stretch of canal in the country, arrive at the locks, cast their eyes across at those enticing circular turrets, and say 'What is it?' Are they gazing upon the dreamy spires of a place of worship, or an infrequently glimpsed Bavarian castle that has been erected only a few miles from Wolverhampton? Or is it something completely different? The answer lies in the fact that this unusually placed and pleasingly ornate structure is a water pumping station, built for the thirsty town of Bilston.

A fine view of the building, showing bartizans (turrets), topped with fish scale tiles

Rapid growth during the industrial revolution meant Bilston's thirst for water had risen dramatically. Wolverhampton council wanted to charge over the odds for their water, so Bilston, with a desire to cut costs, decided to create their own supply. In 1892 a test bore was made right next to Bratch locks and work commenced on the well shafts. Things did not go well (sorry small joke) and the first contractor had to be replaced. Construction of the building was however under way. Two identical steam engines were to be housed inside the building, and technically they are referred to as inverted, vertical, triple expansion units, having 16, 26 and 40in cylinders, with 36in strokes.

James Watt of Birmingham designed and started to make the engines, but problems arose, which resulted in Thornewill & Wareham of Burton upon Trent completing the contract. The two steam engines both drove their own water pump, each one capable of raising one million gallons of water in twenty hours, from a depth of over 700 feet. And this they did until the final shutdown in 1960.

The building was designed and completed by Baldwin Latham of Westminster, for Bilston Urban District Council in 1895, at a cost of £6,133. The station was pumping water to that town, five and a half miles away, twelve months later.

This interior photo, shows Len on the upper level with Victoria, not long after the job had been started. The colossal bulk of the cast iron supporting frame can be clearly seen.

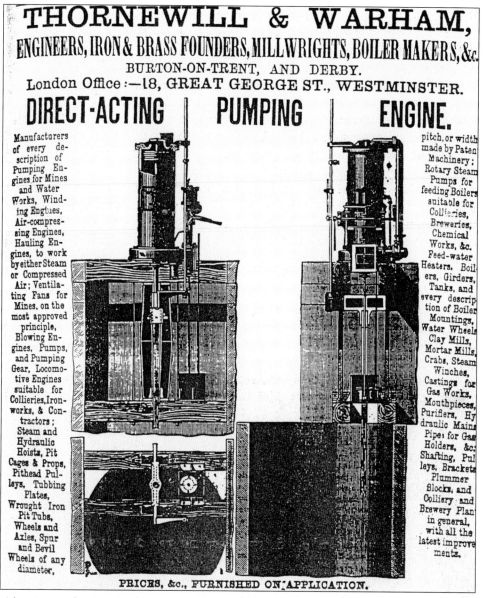

Advertisement from a newspaper, showing the water pumps that were fitted at Bratch. The company
was Thornewill & Warham of Burton upon Trent and Derby. They supplied all manner of
pumping gear to collieries and industry.

The Restoration

After standing idle, silent and forlorn, for a little over thirty years, the powers that be at Severn Trent decided to restore the two magnificent steam engines to their former glory. As you can understand, because of the complete neglect for so long the steam engines, their pumps, and the interior of the building, were in a bit of a state. Filth and debris were everywhere. The water pumps were seized, and the once glittering steelwork was encrusted with a generous dose of rust.

Severn Trent approached Leonard Crane of Wolverhampton, to assess what could be done. Len, now retired, but working harder than ever (showing that you can't keep a skilled man down) is a master of most things mechanical. His speciality however is with steam driven devices. Len has over the years, built and restored his own steam traction engines, and now he spends much of his time taking them to rallies at home and abroad.

Towards the end of 1992 he was given the keys to the pumping station and he went in for 'a recce', as he put it. The sight that greeted him inside that delightful and elaborate brick building could never have been called encouraging. Still, a grand potential was there to be realised and Len rose to the challenge. The size of the undertaking ruled out the restoration of both engines – named *Victoria* and *Alexandra*. Only *Victoria* was to get the full treatment.

Steam Rally and open day at Bratch

In its heyday the pumping station and its two demanding engines were attended by eighteen souls altogether. Divided into three shifts of six men, they had kept it running day and night, thus ensuring that Bilston never ran out of fresh drinking water. The restoration on the other hand was to be accomplished by one expert, one assistant, and a handful of zealous volunteers.

Severn Trent made the initial suggestion to Len, that *Victoria* at least could be run by electricity. 'Certainly not!' replied Len. 'It will have to be steam or nothing. However, we could use compressed air to give it its trial run.' And that's exactly how things were agreed, and a start was made in January of 1993.

Some of the earliest tasks (apart from tidying up the mess) were the removal of the engine's pistons, rings and valves to check them out, clean them and apply a little oil to free things up. They then started to dismantle other moving parts and look at the state of the bearings. After inspection of the water pumps, which are located in the sump of the building, the men discovered that not only were they seized up and corroded, but one of them had been split by frost damage. So they were stripped, and parts from the two made just one good pump. A general 'cannibalising' of one engine was necessary to make the other complete.

To keep the engines running smoothly, each is equipped with a huge flywheel weighing about fourteen tons. Around the circumference of the wheel are a series of square slots, and, by fitting in levers, these act as a manual aid to turn the engine over. After three weeks the team was able with great effort to get the engine to rotate half a turn. It was a start, and when Severn Trent came along for assessment it was enough to encourage them to fund the rest of the work.

By 20 March that year, *Victoria* was ready for testing with the compressed air method, and away she went to the great pleasure and satisfaction of all who were there. For the next three months Len and his team worked hard, stripping, polishing and oiling up, in preparation for the ultimate test of using steam. A large oil-fired boiler, complete with chimney, had to be installed at the back of the building to provide the heat. Unfortunately, the original brick stack had gone, so a rather incongruous cylindrical metal chimney had to be installed. Nevertheless, there are plans to build a brick skin around this anachronism to keep it in tune with the rest of the building, but at the moment expense prohibits such a project.

Some of the internal components of the engine proved to be useless when they were exposed, and they had to be made anew. This entailed the laborious process of producing patterns from which castings could be made. Valves and other parts needed re-machining, and new springs were fitted. Finally, but importantly, *Victoria* received a new paint job, complete with lining. The engine was now ready for steaming, which took place on 14 June 1995.

Since that date there have been scheduled occasional 'Steaming Days', where interested members of the public can go along and experience the living excitement of the engine in action. I attended one of such days in September 1999. So what was it like?

For some years now, I, like so many other visitors to Bratch locks, have admired the building from afar. So I was extremely keen not only to get a closer look at the building, but also to experience a steam engine of this magnitude at work. I paid my entrance fee and strolled up the drive with my wife Jane and daughter Lauren in tow. As we approached the steps and front door, we were amazed to feel the ground pulse beneath our feet as the one engine pounded away some twenty yards distant.

The front entrance to the building has the appearance of a church, with two sets of miniature Corinthian columns, and a pointed Gothic archway. High above us, and on each corner of the building, were two of the four circular turrets (known as bartizans) and between them were the mock battlements. The smart red brick exterior with its tight joints (compare with modern brickwork where the joints are huge) was enhanced by twin, blue brick courses going horizontally around the building. There are areas of purely decorative brickwork that include red, cream and blue engineering bricks. These panels, both square and arched, give striking visual interest from all views.

After taking our fill of the outside we went in. There were already lots of people in there, and the atmosphere was amazing. *Victoria* was pounding rhythmically away, accompanied by great swooshing noises and other thumping sounds. Steam hissed, the flywheel rotated grandly, and all sorts of levers and rods were nodding to and fro in the most hypnotising way. In short the machine was alive, and I was starting to understand the fascination that lovers of all steam engines have. Going up the cast iron stairs we accessed the top of the engine, and the heat increased dramatically. The boiler-suited engineers lovingly attended *Victoria*'s demands for a spot of oil here and a squirt there. I wandered around for some time trying to take it all in and was fortunate enough to bump into someone who kindly explained to me what was going on.

Now perhaps if any of you are wondering where Bilston is getting its water from these days, then glance across the lawn from the pumping station. You will see a small, rather boring, little brick building with all the glamour of a toilet block, and believe me when I tell you that its all going on in there. An electrical pump is now doing all the work, extremely quietly and efficiently, without any assistance, thank you very much. And every now and then a technician comes along to see that all is well, and presses a few buttons. Ah! So much for progress.

I went back to The Bratch two weeks later to get some information from Len. This was no steam day and as we entered the building on a less notable occasion, we were greeted by an eerie silence, everything was still. Was it my imagination, or did *Victoria* look sad? I preferred to imagine that she was silently, but eagerly anticipating the next steaming day, when once again she would come to dynamic life, surrounded by her admirers and attendants. Anyone interested in going to a steam day at Bratch should inquire at Bratch locks.

British Waterways, Bradley Depot

The Ocker Hill depot that had catered for the bulk of the maintenance work for the B.C.N. closed in 1961. Jack Jenkins says that British Waterways received £64,000 for the land, which gave them enough money to design and construct a purpose-built depot at Bradley, and to upgrade to more modern equipment. Of course, I cannot confirm that figure, but certainly the buildings were demolished and the land was developed for a group of high rise flats that came to be known as Boulton Court. The main workshop has no grandiose architectural features, but it is a useful rectilinear structure, with plenty of indoor space. Brian Thompson has been the repair manager for the last twenty years, and in November 1999 he was kind enough to take me on a tour of the facilities. The depot is situated on the old Bradley loop, connecting with the main line at Deepfields Junction, which makes it possible for boats to access the two dry docks. The photograph shows the main building as it was in the 1960s, and there have been few additions since then. The first thing you notice as you drive into the yard are the carefully stacked baulks of timber waiting to be made into lock gates. A couple of maintenance boats were moored in the arm, and there was an old Stewarts & Lloyds tug *Bittel* propped on timbers awaiting repair. Most of the timber in the yard is English Oak, but the carpenters also use a pale yellow wood from the Cameroons called Opepe.

Opepe is a fine grained wood, with excellent characteristics for making lock gates. In days gone by, the Birmingham Canal Navigation owned its own forests, and men would go out to examine the trees before they were felled. Now wood is bought in from suppliers who take their timber from well-managed forests.

The timber is usually felled during the winter months when the sap is at its lowest but, unlike wood for other uses, it does not go through any special seasoning process. We then entered one end of the workshop where a truly enormous lock gate for Diglis (Worcester) was lying horizontally at waist height. It was constructed of a mixture of oak and opepe, and the two woods could be easily distinguished from each other by colour. A lock gate of these huge river proportions takes about three weeks to make, while the much smaller, narrow lock gate can be started and finished in a week.

Since 1961, Bradley has been the maintenance and repair yard for the surviving Midlands canal network, including the remainder of what was the B.C.N., the Staffordshire & Worcester canal, the Stratford, the Birmingham & Worcester, long sections of the Grand Union and the Shropshire Union canal, and the men are even called on at times to construct gates for the Welsh canals. So as you can imagine there is always plenty going on. Presently there are around twenty men working at Bradley, which is approximately the same as at Ocker Hill before it closed. Trades include four carpenters, four boiler makers/welders, two fitters, one electrician and one blacksmith, who has his own area for making pins, hinges, brackets and other miscellaneous ironwork.

Interior of depot showing two docks – rotating dock to the left

After examining the blacksmith's handiwork we went to the other end of the building to view the two dry docks. Lying parallel to each other they resemble two emptied narrow gauge locks, and Brian says they can be filled and emptied in about ten minutes. In the accompanying photo you can just make out a feature of one of those docks which is unique to Britain. When a boat is brought into the dock, the water is emptied away and then it is clamped inside three huge metal rings. Then, by means of an electric motor, the whole boat can be rotated through 360 degrees, which is extremely helpful if the men need to do some welding on the bottom. The Bradley workshop holds open days each year enabling interested persons to go along and see a mix of modern and traditional skills being employed. Thus the vital and highly skilled work undertaken at this busy depot keeps our valuable canal system open and working for all.

On Reflection

The marvellous and enduring quality about the canals is of that they are still with us, and in a speedy, ever changing world it is comforting that some features stay reasonably constant, demonstrating a sense of permanence. Many other features that constituted the industrial revolution, with its blazing furnaces and noisy factories, have been utterly swept away. I am not lamenting the loss of this grimy world, but it was an intriguing chapter in our history, and our grandparents and great grandparents were caught up in it. In the process of change, gigantic steelworks, coal mines, furnaces and foundries, and back to back housing, have been replaced by hi-tech industrial units, glittering shopping malls and featureless urban highways, devoid of pedestrians.

Many miles of canal have been lost forever, many disappearing from the 1950s through to the 1970s, and they can only be found as lines on ageing maps. Thankfully though, due initially to a few small voices crying in the wilderness, many miles have survived to be cruised, walked and appreciated. And now, even the Government, along with enlightened local councils, have awakened to realise what an asset the waterways are, not only to the communities they pass through, but also the country as a whole. British Waterways is working hard to forge new partnerships, to increase funding for the enormous maintenance costs involved in keeping the canals alive. Energetic canal support groups, and local councils are all playing a crucial part in this regeneration programme.

The canal's ability to function and make money, as an important national carrying system has long gone. Its present role is now definitely one of leisure, and the recreational use of the inland waterways has grown by leaps and bounds since the last war. Plus, it is a great teaching aid for history. The canal was designed for work, created work during its existence and will continue to provide work, though of a completely different nature to its original conception. It is just interesting to contrast the changes. Records from the beginning of the canal era shed light on its early occupations and finances. In the 1770s, during the construction of 'Brindley's' Old Main Line, a 'William Mountain' was paid for 'carriage of sundries' and for boating materials. John Lloyd was paid for 'carriage of materials' and for boating bricks, clay and sand, along with Joseph Rowley, Jeremiah Whitehouse and James Jukes. James Place, along with thirty-six other men, was paid the grand sum of £13 8s 1$\frac{1}{2}$d for boating clay. Clay, of necessity, was required in vast quantities for the lining of the canal, its puddling.

How much did a boat cost in those days? Certainly more than the average man could afford, leaving ownership for the most part in the hands of companies. Some did start, and continue to operate with just one boat. In 1770 eight narrow boats were built by the Birmingham Canal Company, at a cost of

£63 each. In 1788, four boats of 70ft by 7ft were built by the Oxford Canal Company at a cost of £70 each. Six years later boats of the same dimensions cost between £90 and £100, showing that inflation has always been with us. Other local tradesmen who supplied materials operated their own horse and carts, but often used a boat belonging to a larger company. On occasions there was a shortage of horses, possibly due to Britain's involvement in a succession of wars. An advert from those years reads 'Such persons are inclined to supply with horses, towing the boats from and to Wednesbury, by trip or journey'.

Slightly more prosperous individuals came to own their own craft and they took great care of their condition and appearance. In time, as trade grew, they acquired one boat after another. By 1795 nearly 30% of boats were owned by only twelve companies, the smallest of which had thirteeen boats.

Into The Present

Nowadays, thousands of people own their own boat, but for far different reasons than those just mentioned. Nevertheless we can definitely say that the use of the canals for leisure and entertainment purposes is not a new phenomenon. In an earlier advertisement featuring Thomas Monk of Tipton, we learned that his packet boat *Euphrates* was available for the private hire of 'parties' on Tuesdays, Wednesdays and Fridays. So not only was Mr Monk an innovator when it came to the development of the cabin, but it appears that he was also one of the first 'Hire Companies.' He operated regular excursions into the limestone caverns under Dudley, and trips to the castle, while other excursions went further afield. One of those early outings was organised by Squire Francis Downing, who was the chief land and mineral agent to the Dudley estates. The purpose of the trip was to take a party from Dudley, to celebrate the opening of the Liverpool & Manchester Railway in September 1830.

Ice boat being worked in the Willenhall area. Probably the same boat seen moored at Sneyd.

In a copy of the *Black Countryman*, Ian Langford writes that Monk's *Euphrates* Packet was a well-built, sleek-hulled craft, much like the fly boats of the time. The horses were colourfully and gaily dressed for special occasions, while the captain, John Jevan, sported a black velvet jockey cap, and starched white shirt, set off with a bright red waistcoat adorned with polished brass buttons. It must have been quite a sight to have watched the *Euphrates* go by during the 1830s.

And our canals and rivers continue to provide new occupations on into modern times. In my local superstore, where the magazine stand contains journals on every subject you can imagine and a few you couldn't I came across four magazines devoted to the subject of inland waterways. After perusing them all, I discovered the format was pretty much the same – a glossy, full colour, well illustrated style, with a range of interesting waterway related articles, surrounded by an enormous quantity of advertisements.

One of those magazines (which I will not name) comprised 120 pages, sixty-two of which were dedicated to advertising this is not a criticism by the way, just an observation. In other words, just over 50% of that magazine was designed to lure prospective punters into parting with their cash on boats, services or holidays. Of those sixty-two pages I found fifty-seven adverts for boat hire firms, twelve for marinas offering their services, an amazing forty-five boat building companies, and fifty-eight adverts for accessories and services.

Back in 1998 I happened to visit one of those boat building companies, Stow Hill Marine, which was was pleasantly situated on the banks of the Grand Union canal. Dave Hill gave me an enjoyable tour of their impressive boat building operations and I was able to see the whole process from the delivery of the sheet steel at 6 and 10mm thickness, through to the finished product. The almost completed boat in the covered dock was luxuriously kitted out, with its light oak decor, tongue and grooved internal boarding and quality finish.

The cost of a boat at that time was approximately about £1,000 per foot and this particular boat was a 65-footer, so it was pretty easy to estimate the final cost. Dave pointed out that they were an extremely busy company and their waiting list was around two years. All of these figures go to prove that leisure on Britain's canals and rivers is a big and booming business. Hopefully a positive sign for the years to come.

F.M.C. Depot Birmingham 1999.

The Black Country Living Museum

Carefully preserving the past is the ever expanding Black Country Museum, with its colliery, village and iron company. Its location in Tipton is perfect for many reasons. Not only is the replica of the 1712 Newcomen engine (see picture on page 118) near its original location, but the grounds are positioned around an interesting, historical canal site that includes the entrance to the Dudley tunnel, as well as a short arm that leads to the early limestone kilns.

Oral Histories

The interviews that laid the basis for the life experiences of the canal folk were very time consuming but extremely enjoyable, and I learned such a lot from just listening to these lovely people. As time goes by, prospective interviewees are getting harder to find and, sadly on occasions, after making a phone call, or knocking a door, I discovered that so and so had not long died, and that it was a shame that I hadn't called six months earlier. It also became apparent early on in my research that surviving memories didn't go back much further than the Second World War. I was therefore looking for people at least sixty-five years old or hopefully older. The difficulty with probing people's minds (in the nicest possible way) is that memories naturally fade as the years take their toll, and facts get confused. But it was equally amazing how a photograph, map or diagram could evoke a hidden wealth of information.

One person that I missed by about a year was George Wood, the husband of Margaret. However I found it quite easy to build up a picture of this truly jolly individual by looking at photographs, talking to his wife, and listening to recorded conversations with him as he chatted about his work on his beloved Staffordshire and Worcestershire canal. At seventy years of age his wife Margaret is bright and active, has a clear memory, and works hard to keep her home immaculately. I was initially worried that she would get upset as we listened to these recorded memories of her husband talking (she hadn't played them since George's death). But Margaret is a wonderful lady and in some way I am sure that she gained some real comfort when she heard his chuckling voice George was a constant chuckler.

Above: A Typical Black Country scene. Boats at the Iron Works.
Below: Two boats with their individual sign writing. F.M.C. at the back, while the Samuel Barlow cabin has recieved a round window at some stage.

Many years before, I discovered that George and Margaret had been interviewed by students from a local university, who had undertaken oral histories as part of their course. It was apparent while listening to the tapes that the interviewers knew little about canals and I think the mistake they made was to be unspecific with their questions. So if you are going to do any oral interviews, you have to do your homework and know your subject first. Try not to use broad questions like 'What was it like on the canals?' You need instead to use pointed questions such as 'What was your horse's name? What did you have for breakfast before you started work?' and 'What was your gaffer like?', and then I am sure you will bring those memories back to mind and thus have a better result. Also don't forget to show tact and be respectful.

I had a rather lucky day when I went over to Bumble Hole and Windmill End, for I discovered in one location, not one, but three elderly men who had interesting connections with the canals. They tended to meet in the afternoon at the newly-built visitor centre for tea and biscuits. I must add at this point though that I had been warned about one of these individuals. The comment went something like 'I don't know if you'll get much out of Jack. He can be a bit of a funny bugger at times'. So I approached the three potential interviewees with great caution. My initial objective was just to introduce myself, tell them what I was doing, and leave it at that. Sometimes with Black Country folk you just can't wade in as though you've been buddies for years, you have to take relationships slowly, a bit at a time. And so it was that I met William, Joe and Jack for the first time. Joe was immediately friendly, William was very quiet and almost shy, but Jack was running true to form.

A view through the lifting bridge, toward the purpose built boat dock.

*Copy of 1712
Steam Pumping
Engine B.C.
Museum.*

When I told them I was collecting experiences about the canals from the past, his reply was. 'Yoh doh want to remember that load of rubbish, it was bad enough at the time'. I beat a hasty retreat. After a couple of weeks I returned to the centre on a sunny afternoon, they were sitting at a table outside, taking tea and watching the world, the boats and the swans go by. I pulled up a chair and joined them. My plan was to ignore Jack and talk to the other two. Joe has a quick mind and an active memory. I started to fill my notepad with information from him and the occasional snippet from William. Jack said nothing for quite some time, but after a while he was unable to resist making a few comments and got more and more involved as the afternoon progressed. The summer passed by and I made the occasional trip to the visitor centre in order to carry on the discussions, but also on later dates to verify what I had written.

Earlier in the year I started out with a tape recorder and notepad, but I learned that some people are put off by the presence of such a gadget and it makes an interview too formal. My taped conversation really came to an end at Phil Garret's home, when the machine fell on the floor with a thump and a twang. It never worked after that, so I went back to pen and paper.

Jack mellowed as the weeks went by and he related to me his days in the army. Jack is one of a dwindling group that went all the way through the Second World War and came back alive. Most of his time was spent in the desert fighting Rommel. Jack has the scars to prove it. I came to realise that his external 'crotchety nature' was caused by old age and the pain he was suffering from arthritic joints. He usually brought his little dog along to the centre for an outing, and in a top pocket he always had a few wrapped sweets. One afternoon, after we had been chatting, he furtively took one of these sweets out of his pocket, and slid it toward me across the table, as though someone might catch us in the act. I knew from then on that Jack was a big softy at heart.

For Jack and his contemporaries in the 1950s, carrying work on the canals was coming to a close, but it amazes me that, in the middle of the twentieth century, horses could still be seen pulling the rare boat. The Dudley tunnel was receiving yearly checks, and one of Joe's jobs was to enter it using the ice boat *Fram*, to 'dip' the water level. One of the last people to use that tunnel in any commercial way was Jack Wheeler, and he had his own little tricks for getting his boats through that long black tube. Towards the end of the day, he would take his boats into the Tipton end of the tunnel, loaded with coal for the Harts Hill Iron Works, and leave them there. He would go over to Park Head locks at the opposite end and open one of the paddles. The gentle, but continual flow of water would, during the course of the night, slowly flush his boats through like sticks in a drainpipe. Things didn't always work out for Jack though, sometimes his boats would get stuck, and he would have to go in to retrieve them.

The one room gauging office at Park Head, yards from the southern end of the tunnel, was dismantled in 1949. Its last gauging attendant was another Jack (Jack Woodhouse) and the brickwork from this building helped to fill in part of the adjacent Pensnett canal, which had been stopped off some time earlier.

All things considered, most of the people I met while doing the research for this book, were extremely helpful, not only for information, but also with photographs. Some of the photographs were not only interesting but touching too. In one book, for instance, I came across a picture of Colin William's father from about thirty years ago (Colin didn't realise that a photograph of his father existed). When I showed it to him, he stared at it for what seemed ages and said 'Yep that's him all right'. Which just proves that a little digging can provoke an emotional response at times. A few weeks later, I came across photographs of the inside of the Ocker Hill, B.C.N. depot, which was a great surprise because I didn't realise any existed, and it was all very exciting.

I must finally add that without the early back-breaking work of the navvies, there would be no canals to talk about. They are the unsung heroes of the inland waterways, or are they? In Stourport in the 1960s there was a folk group who included in their repertoire, a song about the navvies that seems a fitting end to this book, and a tribute to them, and I shall repeat it in full. It was written by Ian Campbell and Tony Baylis, though I have been unable to trace either of these two gentlemen to supply the music to go with the lyrics. But the words do the job perfectly.

I am a navigational man, and I come from County Cork.
I had to leave me native home, to find a job of work.
The crops were bad in Ireland, and the tax too much to pay,
So here I am in England, digging up the waterway.

CHORUS

Here come the navvies, out to earn their pay,
We work with barrow, plough and spade, to clear the cut away,
And when we put the puddle in, with sweat we wet the clay,
And we scar the face of England, for to make the waterway.

Now once I was a ploughman, and I did a decent job,
I worked from dawn to darkness, just to earn my couple of bob.
But when the praties died on us, I couldn't pay me way,
So here I am in England, digging up the waterway.

We work up in the mountains, and we work down on the plains,
We work out in all weathers, in the wind and snow and rain.
The going isn't easy, cutting highways through the rocks,
We mark our way with aqueducts, with tunnels and with locks.

The lads who build the waterways, they are a motley crew,
And when we've sweated all day long, we like a drink or two,
The local folks don't take to us, but still I'm proud to say,
In years to come, our monument will be the waterway.

References

The Birmingham Canal Navigation's. Broadbridge, S.
The Black Countryman – The Magazine of the Black Country Society.
Towpath Guide. Staffs & Worcestershire Canal. Langford, J.I.
Canals of the West Midlands, Hadfield. C.
James Brindley, Engineer. Boucher, C.
F.M.C. A short History of Fellows. Faulkner, A.
Clayton's of Oldbury. Faulkner, A.
The History of The Horseley Company. Allen, J
The Waters of Birmingham. Jones
The Building of the Dudley Canal Tunnel. Langford, J.I.
Industrial Canal—The Coal Trade. Shill, R..
Cobbs Engine House. Price, G.
The Canal Boatmen 1760 – 1914. Hansen, Harry

Followin' the Osses – A manuscript by Phil Clayton.

Canal Societies.

The Birmingham Canal Navigation's Society (B.C.N.S.)
The Staffordshire and Worcestershire Canal Society
The Dudley Canal Trust. Blowers Green Pump House, Peartree Lane Dudley, DY2 OXP. 01384 236275.

Other Tempus canal and inland waterway titles include:

The Aire & Calder Navigation
Mike Clarke in association with the Waterways Museum at Goole
0 7524 1715 0   £9.99

The Arun Navigation
Paul Vine
0 7524 2103 4   £9.99

The Gloucester & Sharpness Canal
Hugh Conway-Jones
0 7524 1709 6   £10.99

Leeds & Liverpool Canal In Yorkshire
Dr Gary Firth
0 7524 1631 6   £9.99

To Maintain and Improve: A History of the Lower Avon Navigation Trust
D.H. Burlingham
0 7524 1756 8   £14.99

The River Trent Navigation
Mike Taylor
0 7524 1743 6   £9.99

The Wey & Arun Junction Canal
P.A.L. Vine
0 7524 1721 5   £9.99

The Wilts & Berks Canal
Doug Small
0 7524 1619 7   £9.99